UISTS & BARRA

The author thanks those who gave
assistance with the sourcing of some of
the local details which appear herein.
Special thanks to Eric Shaw who
transformed the author's raw text into
disc format.

CONTENTS

Half-title: The waters and sandy beach of Bagh Siar on Vatersay Island

Title page: Orosay, South Uist

Left: The island of Vatersay and Cornaig Bay, Barra

INTRODUCING THE ISLANDS

THE ISLANDS WHICH ARE the subject of this book are part of the Hebridean chain of islands which form the local government area known as the Western Isles. The Southern Isles include North Uist, Benbecula, South Uist, joined together by causeway and bridge, and Barra, accessible from South Uist and the Scottish mainland (Oban in Argyll) by roll-on roll-off car ferry. In addition there are smaller islands of significant size which support populations: Berneray in the Sound of Harris, Eriskay linked to South Uist by ferry, and Vatersay which is now joined to Barra by a causeway.

Even a cursory glance at the map will reveal one of the problems of island living: inter-island access. Up until the 1940s the islands were wholly dependent on small cargo ships delivering lifeline essentials and exporting the island produce. These ships, called 'puffers', were built with flat bottoms so that they could be stranded deliberately on the sandy beaches and stony shores to discharge their cargo. Travelling between the islands of North Uist, Benbecula and South Uist meant hiring a horse-drawn cart to take one across the fords at low tides, accompanied by an expert guide. The

Above: Loch Yeor, one of the many lochs on the fretted coastline of North Uist

Left: One of the few thatched crofter houses at Malaclete, North Uist

7

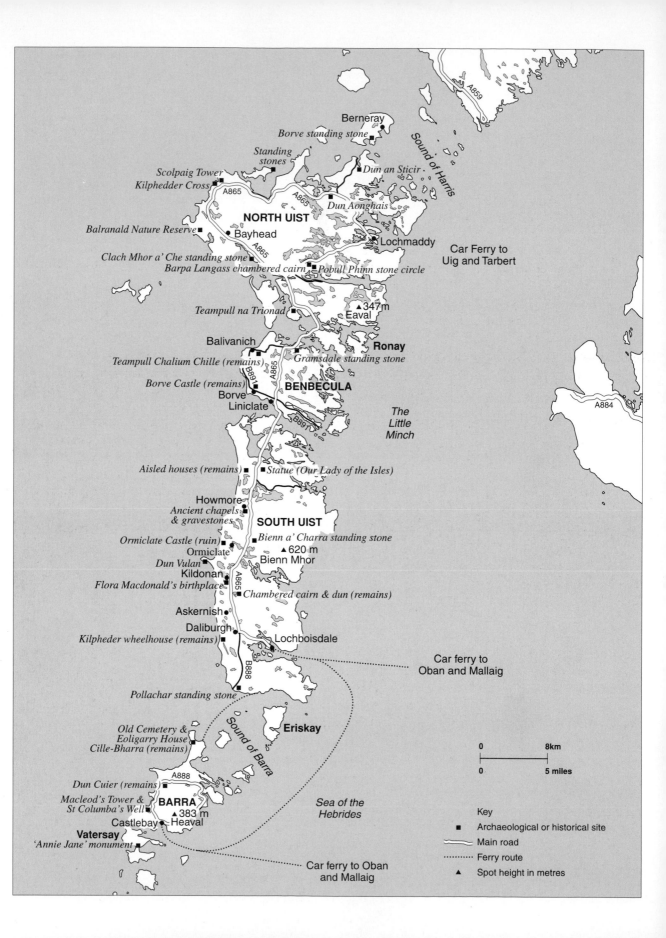

Berneray

Borve standing stone

*Standing
stones*

Scolpaig Tower
Kilphedder Cross

■ *Dun an Sticir*

A865   A865

Dun Aonghais

NORTH UIST

Balranald Nature Reserve ■
● Bayhead

● Lochmaddy

A865

Car Ferry to
Uig and Tarbert

Clach Mhor a' Che standing stone ■
Barpa Langass chambered cairn ■ ■ *Pobull Phinn stone circle*

Teampull na Trionad ■
▲347m
Eaval

Balivanich ●
Teampull Chalium Chille (remains) ■   *Gramsdale standing stone*

Ronay

A865

Borve Castle (remains) ■
Borve ■
Liniclate ●

B891

BENBECULA

B891

*The
Little
Minch*

A884

Aisled houses (remains) ■   ■ *Statue (Our Lady of the Isles)*

Howmore ●
*Ancient chapels
& gravestones* ■

SOUTH UIST

Ormiclate Castle (ruin) ■
Ormiclate ●
Dun Vulan ■
Kildonan ●
Flora Macdonald's birthplace

Bienn a' Charra standing stone ■
▲620 m
Bienn Mhor

■ *Chambered cairn & dun (remains)*

Askernish ●
Daliburgh ●
Kilpheder wheelhouse (remains) ■

● Lochboisdale

A865

Car ferry to
Oban and Mallaig

B888

Pollachar standing stone ■

Eriskay

Sound of Barra

*Old Cemetery &
Eoligarry House* ■
Cille-Bharra (remains)

A888

Dun Cuier (remains) ■

*Macleod's Tower &
St Columba's Well* ■

BARRA
▲383 m
Castlebay ● ▲Heaval

*Sea of the
Hebrides*

0   8km

0   5 miles

Vatersay
'Annie Jane' monument ■

Car ferry to Oban
and Mallaig

Key

■   Archaeological or historical site

   Main road

·········   Ferry route

▲   Spot height in metres

dangers inherent in these ford crossings were summed up in the Gaelic prayer, *Faothail mhath dhuibh* (A good ford to you).

Today, inter-island travel is much less hazardous. In 1943 Benbecula and South Uist ceased to be independent islands when the South Bridge was opened. The older generation still call it 'O'Regan's Bridge' in remembrance of Father O'Regan who campaigned for the link. In reality his case was consolidated by the fact that there was a need, during the war years, of a link between Lochboisdale in South Uist, and the RAF aerodrome at Balivanich in Benbecula. The connection between Benbecula and North Uist was opened in 1960 by Her Majesty the Queen Mother. Thus the three main islands were provided with a through route of 70 miles (112km) from the Sound of Berneray off North Uist, and Pollachar in South Uist, a route which can now be enjoyed by locals and visitors alike. It is, however, not a high-speed facility. Much of the road is single-track which requires the judicious use of passing-places but which also allows the motorist to enjoy the slow-moving scenery.

THE ISLANDS

ALTHOUGH THE ISLANDS in the southern chain of the Western Isles share a common pool of economies, public services, methods of land use, climate, natural history, and a strong cultural and linguistic heritage based on the Gaelic language, each has a definite claim to some individual distinction. History and pre-history, religion, clan affiliations, nineteenth-century experiences with unsympathetic landlords, clearances and forced emigrations, have all made their impact on the people of the islands in different ways so that each community has emerged into the light of the present day with a characteristic identity.

NORTH UIST

This is the largest island, about 13 miles (21km) north to south and about 18 miles (29km) across east to west at its widest. The land encompasses a rather complex pattern of freshwater lochs, all providing good fishing for anglers. It has been estimated that these lochs make up one-third of the island mass. Loch Scadavay is the largest one with a shoreline reckoned to run some 50 miles (80km). The depth of Loch Obisiray is 151ft (46m) and is overlooked by the 1,139ft (347m) height of Eaval. The eastern coastline of the island is the more rugged and is serrated by long intrusions of the sea. In fact the long arm of the sea, Loch Eport, reaches across the island so far inland that its head is less than half a mile (0.8km) from Loch Oban a' Chlachain, thus being defeated in its intent to create a separate island of the southern part of North Uist. South of Lochmaddy, North Lee (821ft/850m) and South Lee (898ft/274m) rise

CROFTERS' HOSTELS

Throughout the Western Isles there are simple hostels run by the Gatliff Hebridean Hostels Trust. They provide very basic accommodation for short-stay backpackers and are intended for visitors who wish to become acquainted with the crofting communities, Gaelic language and culture and the natural environment of the islands. One hostel (thirty-six beds) is located at Lochmaddy, North Uist (NF 918 687) which is open from mid-May to the end of September. Another is located next to the ancient chapel and graveyard at Howmore in South Uist (NF 757 365) with eight beds. It is a white stone building with a thatched roof and is open all year round. A third (twelve beds) is on the island of Berneray, North Uist, at a place marked 'Baile' (NF 932 814) on the OS map. Contact the Trust Secretary at 30 Francis Street, Stornoway, Lewis.

SIGNPOSTING IN GAELIC

When the Western Isles Council was formed in 1975 under the re-organisation of Local Government in Scotland, a commitment was made to give the Gaelic language a high profile in public life. One aspect of this policy was to have road signs in both Gaelic and English initially but then to establish the use of Gaelic only. Thus, the visitor will be confronted with the names of crofting townships in their Gaelic equivalents. Those who are used to seeing the names of places on the Continent in the language of a particular country will be familiar with the manner in which one can move round the islands without getting lost: using the latest Ordnance 'Landranger' Survey maps. In the Southern Isles the road system is not complex and it takes no great degree of intelligence to work out the places at which one stops or drives through.

One map has been specially designed with bilingual names of places and is readily available at the Tourist Offices in Lochmaddy (Pier Road), Lochboisdale (Pier Road) and Castlebay (Main Street). Most Gaelic place-names tend to have a near-equivalent English: Loch nam Madadh (Lochmaddy), Cladach Chirceboist (Claddach Kirkibost), Solas (Sollas), Creag Ghoraidh (Creagorry), Lionacleit (Linaclete), Loch Baghasdail (Lochboisdale), Cille Pheadair (Kilphedar), and Bagh a Chaisteil (Castlebay).

together to form a spectacular mass which is bare, angular and isolated.

Equally spectacular is the west coast of North Uist, in sharp contrast to the hilly moorland of the eastern side of the island. Here lie the greener lands of the machair, a fertile plain built up from shell-sand, the product of thousands of years of Atlantic waters grinding up the calcareous remnants of prehistoric sea creatures. And here is where the bulk of the island's population lives, in crofting townships.

BENBECULA

The meaning of Benbecula in Gaelic is *Beinn a' bh-fhaodhla*, the Mountain of the Fords. The island is the flattest in the Southern Isles and the mountain is the rather presumptuous Rueval, 407ft (124m) in height. Like its northern neighbour, the east coast is deeply serrated and the main ground mass is littered with freshwater lochs, with the west side of the island rather flat and lying on machair soil. Its importance is due to the main urban centre at Balivanich. Here the sprawling buildings of the British Army have created a small town next to the airport, both of which have tended to act as a magnet for a number of industrial and commercial enterprises, including the Southern Isles offices of the Western Isles Council. A little to the south of Balivanich is Lionacleit, where an impressive community school now serves the young population of the vicinity. The school also accommodates a theatre, a museum and a swimming pool, all used by locals and visitors.

During the last century Benbecula was a Mecca for sportsmen, out bagging seals along the shores and much wildlife in the hinterland of the island. Their pursuits did not go down well with the crofters as one hunting visitor discovered. He wrote, 'Much of the pleasure in shooting in the Outer Hebrides is spoilt by the conduct of the crofters. It is not conducive to sport to be followed by a gang of men and ordered out of the country, nor is it pleasant to be cursed in Gaelic by a crowd of irate old women, even if you do not understand every word they say. They accuse us of shooting their horses and sheep, filled in the pits we dug in the sandhills for geese, shouted out to up the geese we were stalking, cut the canvas and broke the seats of our folding-boat, and tried in every way to spoil our sport'.

That attitude of the crofters to the visiting sportsmen was understandable. They tramped over corn fields, disturbed livestock and acted with an arrogance bred out of superiority. These days, anglers and birdwatchers, walkers and backpackers have a greater respect for their surroundings and are aware of the fact that the land is a working area for crofters, their crops and their animals.

The main road on Benbecula runs from Gramsdale in the north, round the coast to Balivanich and Lionacleit in the south. Another road runs from Gramsdale through Market Stance to Creagorry, something of a short-cut if one's time is limited to get to South Uist. Two lateral roads take one to Peter's Port and Uiskevagh, and require careful driving.

SOUTH UIST

The Benbecula War Memorial looking towards the hills of South Uist

This island is some 22 miles (35km) long and roughly 8 miles (13km) across east to west. The main road, north to south, runs through the populated areas on the west side of the island where the machair land is to be found. The eastern side of South Uist is mostly desolate moorland fringed by a rocky coastline and backed by three groups of hills. The southern group lies between Loch Boisdale and the southern end of South Uist. The highest peak is Easaval, a modest 800ft (244m), with its companions Roneval at 660ft (200m) and Marava at 530ft (160m).

Between Loch Boisdale and Loch Eynort a second group takes in ten hills, each distinct and with two exceeding 1,000ft (305m) in height. They are mostly covered with grass or heather. The third group lays claim to the principal summits in South Uist: Beinn Mhor (2,033ft/620m) and Hecla (1,990ft/606m), a rather handsome and shapely rise which has a grassy ridge leading to the subsidiary peak of Cas fo Thuath (1,154ft/352m). Just south of the Cas is Glen Corrodale, from which a stream empties into Corrodale Bay. This is a remote spot, reasonably accessible to determined walkers, where Prince Charles Edward hid for several weeks during the summer of 1746, avoiding the frantic searches for him and his companions

The dramatic scene looking over Lochs Hamasclett and Druidibeg to the rise of Beinn Mhor (2,034ft/620m) on South Uist

Stacking newly cut peat on South Uist for winter fuel

Overleaf: The beach near Borve, on the west coast of Barra, at Halaman Bay

TREASURE ISLAND

Until the middle years of the last century, a story deeply embedded in the folk memory of the people of Barra told of a treasure ship which was wrecked off the island in 1728. Tales of barrels seen lying at the bottom of the sea filled with gold, silver and jewels added no little spice to the yarn. Many dismissed the tale as a product of fertile imagination. However, truth is often stranger than fiction.

In May 1728 a certain Alexander MacKenzie, a Principal Clerk of Session in Edinburgh, and who held a commission as 'Admiral of the Long Island' (the Western Isles), heard about a wreck near Barra. He immediately sent a trustworthy person to Barra to get some details, on the basis of which he arranged for the salvage of the wreck. A vessel was purchased and the services of a Captain Jacob Row were engaged who was well known for his salvage work, along with his crew of experienced divers. The crew were advised to arm themselves with 'travelling weapons' for fear that the Barra natives might create a disturbance.

Work on the wreck was difficult, owing to the conditions of the sea, but Captain Row and MacKenzie seemed to be satisfied with what they discovered. In the meantime, the Dutch East India Company were looking into the fate of one of their ships. This vessel, the Adelaar, *had sailed in March 1728 for the Dutch East Indies and*

(continued opposite)

by English ships in the Minch waters. From the top of Beinn Mhor, and on a good day, freaks of image can throw up the distant hills of Northern Ireland some 100 miles (160km) to the south.

BARRA

The island of Barra is the most westerly inhabited island in Great Britain. Less than 40 square miles (100 sq km) in extent it can lay claim to more than 1,000 species of wild plants growing in its varied, and often spectacular, topography. Over 150 species of birds have been recorded. Barra is about 8 miles (13km) long and 7 miles (11km) wide, which might give the impression that a quick visit is all that is needed if one is an island-bagger. But Barra epitomises all that is best in the Western Isles: clean beaches, an

Halaman Bay on the west side of Barra

(continued)
Batavia and then into oblivion. The ship's cargo included ingots of silver, bags of silver coins, bars of gold and other valuables.

Convinced that MacKenzie had recovered the ship's cargo, the Company took him to court in Edinburgh. For his part, MacKenzie claimed that there was no proof that the ship belonged to the Company and that it was easy for any firm anywhere to declare that they had lost a ship containing valuable cargo. The court case ran on for four years until 1732 when the Company obtained a decree against MacKenzie for £2,470. MacKenzie's expenses in recovering goods from the wreck came to nearly £14,000, a sum which was, coincidentally, the amount that the Dutch Company maintained was the value of the precious cargo.

Whether MacKenzie did in fact manage to recover the gold, silver and coin from the wreck was never quite established. But it is interesting that MacKenzie and Captain Jacob Row later went to Mull to carry out salvage work on the Spanish Armada galleon which sank near Tobermoray, though that venture was a complete failure.

invigorating climate, a dominating seascape and great walking opportunities. The highest peak is Heaval (1,260ft/384m) on top of which there is a statue in Carrara marble of the Blessed Virgin and Child, erected during the Marian Year in 1954. It overlooks the main town of Castlebay.

THE OTHER ISLANDS

There are three main satellite islands in the Southern Isles, each supporting a significant population. Berneray lies snugly at the western end of the Sound of Harris and is soon to be connected to North Uist by a causeway. Eriskay, served by a small car ferry, is at the southern tip of South Uist. Vatersay, off the east side of Barra, has had a causeway built to serve its population who can now enjoy the services and delights of Castlebay.

ISLAND POPULATIONS

A policeman's lot: off-duty feeding time for lambs at Lochmaddy Police Station

THE DATA FROM THE 1991 Census has revealed a slow decline in the population figures for the islands in the southern chain, though the decline is now less dramatic than in times past. During the early years of last century each island experienced significant population rises as the result of the kelp industry (burning seaweed to produce ash). In the 1820s, when this industry foundered, the islanders were forced to depend on whatever living they could make off their land, over which they had no security of tenure. To say that times were hard is an understatement. The development of the fishing industry in the 1850s, which lasted until World War I, helped to alleviate the situation, with many crofters benefiting from the herring fishing. When that declined, islanders found themselves once again dependent on their own resources. Those who found it impossible to support their families emigrated to the Scottish mainland and to new lives overseas.

The population of Barra for most of last century was around the 2,500 mark. By 1931 this figure was 2,300, falling to 1,600 thirty years later. The present figure is 1,316.

The maximum population figure for South Uist, 7,300, occurred in 1841 – the result of the increase in population working in the kelp industry. By 1861, some 3,000 people had left the island, many forcibly shipped to Canada. Thereafter the rise in prosperity created by the herring industry tended to increase the population to 4,300 by 1891. But then the island suffered a gradual decline to 2,285 in 1991. Whether that figure can be stabilised will depend on how well the various island-based development agencies can introduce meaningful economic activities to allow families to stay in South Uist.

Benbecula has never had a large population. The maximum figure, 1,700, occurred in 1881. By 1951, 700 people lived on Benbecula. The advent of the Army rocket-testing facility at Ichodar on South Uist boosted that figure to 1,300 by 1961 and is at present holding steady at 1,803, reflecting the fact that Benbecula is an economic energy centre attracting people from other parts of the Southern Isles.

The maximum population of North Uist occurred in 1821, a figure of 5,000, which again reflected the contribution which the kelp industry made on the factors which influenced population increase. Thereafter there was a gradual decline, with the herring industry contributing a couple of 'highs' at the turn of the century. The present figure is 1,815.

The main factors which have effected the downward trend in the islands' populations have been the clearances, the potato famine in the 1850s, the decline in the kelp industry, a continued state of insecurity (stabilised by the 1886 Crofters Act which gave security of tenure to crofters), lack of meaningful economic development, and a desire on the part of the islanders to make a better life for themselves elsewhere.

GETTING TO THE ISLANDS

The car ferry from Oban, the Lord of the Isles, *loading at Castlebay Pier, with Kismul Castle in the background*

THE ISLANDS ARE CONNECTED to the Scottish mainland and the rest of the world by both sea and air, and they are also inter-connected so that island-hopping adds that extra dimension of interest to any visit.

There are ferries from the mainland. Lochmaddy, in North Uist, is on the run (under two hours) from the terminal in Uig on the island of Skye. Both Castlebay in Barra and Lochboisdale on South Uist are connected to the terminal at Oban in Argyll by a ferry which does a triangular trip. The sailing time from Oban to Castlebay is just over five hours with one and a half hours to make the second leg from Castlebay to Lochboisdale before the ferry returns to Oban. During the summer months a ferry connection is available to Lochboisdale and Castlebay from Mallaig (taking about three and a half hours).

Inter-island ferry connections are: Harris to North Uist (one hour ten minutes); Berneray to North Uist (fifteen minutes); South Uist to Eriskay (fifteen minutes).

Air links leave Glasgow Airport to arrive on Barra after an hour's flying time. With the inter-island flight services, Barra is linked to Benbecula (forty minutes) and to Stornoway on Lewis (thirty-five minutes).

The car ferry Hebridean Isles *at Lochmaddy Pier. Launched in 1985 at just over 3,000 tonnes, she connects Tarbert, Harris and Uig in Skye*

A round-up of seaweed, near Kallin, North Uist. The weed is air-dried before being transported to the Scottish mainland for processing to produce alginic acid. It is then used in cosmetics, ice-cream and pharmaceutical products

Right: The relatively new harbour at Kallin, on the island of Grimsay, North Uist, provided by the Local Authority to provide much needed facilities for local fishermen

ISLAND ECONOMIES

THE MAIN SHEET-ANCHORS of the economy of the islands are crofting and fishing, with the latter concentrated on shellfish. Fish-farming is a sector gaining in economic importance and offering useful employment to those who supplement their crofting incomes with other types of activity. With the presence of the Royal Artillery Range Hebrides, centred on Balivanich on Benbecula, a community of around 700 people (troops and their families) has boosted the provision of services and facilities to the local population in the island and on both the Uists. The presence in Benbecula of Local Government offices has also provided much-needed employment, often on a full-time basis.

With the advent of the age of computers, an increasing number of people are now working from home in 'tele-cottages', providing services for mainland companies. The construction industry, haulage and transport and servicing all contribute to the fairly wide economic base and offer an essential degree of stability for families who have opted to stay in the islands.

THE CHRISTMAS TRIBUTE

It was a traditional belief in the Uists that Christ had once commanded Peter and the apostles to row 707 strokes out from the shore to cast their nets. There they would find fish that contained the tribute money to be given as alms for the poor. For many generations, until the late 1800s, fishermen performed the same act by rowing 707 strokes out into the Atlantic. All fish caught were then distributed among the poorest in the community.

Another tradition was that the two black spots on each side of the haddock, above the pectoral fin, were the marks which St Peter made as he picked up the fish to reveal the tribute coins in its mouth. In the Uists the name for a haddock was iasg Pheadail, *Peter's fish, a term still used among the older generation of fishermen.*

1 ISLAND SEASCAPES

View from Loch Yeor on the coastal road to Loch Portain, north of Lochmaddy

IT MIGHT BE STATING the obvious that when one is on an island, one is more than conscious of the fact that the sea is a dominant factor. Its influence is all-pervading and has been for many thousands of years and more, back into geological times when the whole of the Western Isles comprised a cliff-backed platform and the sea-level was some thirty feet higher than it is at present. Under the process of glacial erosion this platform was reformed a number of times with the surface being added to by large quantities of erosion products such as lodgement till. Inevitably, during the three main glacial periods, the last around 10,000 years ago, the coastal outlines of the Southern Isles were changed to create the present-day variety which is quite outstanding, so much so that the whole of the Outer Hebrides is seen by some as an area of environmental significance.

What is of great interest is the evidence of submerged features of terrestrial origin which are regularly found under the sea, including tree stumps and the remains of submerged peat beds. It has been suggested by geologists that the whole chain of the Western Isles is sinking slowly into the sea, as evidenced by sea encroachment identified at more than twenty locations in the islands. One of these is at Bagh na Croabhag (Bay of Small Trees) on the tidal island of Vallay, off North Uist, where inter-tidal peat deposits contain birch stumps *in situ*.

The range of coastal features seen as one travels through the Uists and Barra includes shores which are muddy, sandy, rocky, shingle and salt-marsh. Added to these are such features as the sand dunes, machair and vertical cliffs. Inevitably, these softer features, such as the sand dunes, are undergoing constant change particularly on the western coastal areas where breaking waves from the stormy Atlantic in winter months are evidence of the creative sculpturing art of Nature itself.

But what are undoubtedly breathtaking are the vast stretches of sand as seen to the north-west of North Uist, at Vallay Strand and the Traigh Ear, and all down the west coast of Benbecula, South Uist and to the west and north of Barra. The latter, the Traigh Mhor, is unusual on account of the number of cusp-shaped ridges composed entirely of empty cockle shells. This beach also serves as the only airport in the British Isles where aircraft landing and take-off times are controlled by tidal conditions. Within recent years something in the region of 600 tonnes of cockle shells were extracted per annum from the beach for processing at the building close by, where the author Sir Compton MacKenzie (of *Whisky Galore* fame) once lived.

One of the finest storm shingle ridges anywhere in Britain can be seen at Aird in Benbecula. It is still prone to shape-shifting when the high tides combine with wild storms to throw large boulders some distance up to the higher reaches of the beach.

It is the machair lands on the west coasts of the islands, however, which have made it possible for the population to prosecute an agricultural activity which not only maintains the economic and social stability of the many crofting townships but also ensures the continuity of their cultural and linguistic heritage.

Machair, recognised as a peculiar and almost unique landform, has been defined by the Joint Nature Conservation Committee as: 'Gently sloping coastal plains formed by wind-blown calcareous shell-sand, which incorporates a mosaic of species-rich grassland, fens and lochs, with dunes towards the sea and blackland (a mixture of peat and sand) further inland. All these individual elements are crucial parts of the machair system. The grassland has traditionally been maintained by low intensity agriculture. In Europe this habitat occurs only in Scotland and Ireland'.

However, it is not just the physical make-up of machair that has made it an unusual European landform. The climate is an influential

WHISKY GALORE

In February 1941 the 12,000 tonne cargo ship Politician *went aground off the tiny island of Calway, at the eastern end of the Sound of Eriskay. Her navigator had mistaken Eriskay Sound for the Sound of Barra. She had a mixed cargo, which included some 24,000 cases of whisky intended for the American market. At a time of scarcity of the amber liquid, known as 'the cratur', it attracted the attention of the people of the Uists and Barra and many cases were rescued from the ship, even after it was declared an irrecoverable wreck. Some of the men were arrested and brought before the Sheriff at Lochmaddy and sentenced to terms of imprisonment of up to two months for offences against the excise laws.*

The incident provided the plot for a book and the film Whisky Galore *by Sir Compton MacKenzie. It was filmed on Barra and at Castlebay. In 1997 a bottle of 'Politician' whisky was sold for over £1,500, even though its contents were not drinkable.*

Overleaf: Looking up from Blashaval over Loch Blashaval and North and South Lee

23

factor in that the shell-sand can only blow from the beaches inland with typical strong winds, and there must be sufficient moisture to trap the sand. These two elements are essential to maintain the machair system, to produce a balance between damaging erosion and deposition.

In addition, there is the all-important human factor: the manner in which the machair has been managed, probably from the earliest times of human settlement to the present day. Both grazing and selected rotational cultivation have always been carried out in accordance with long-standing traditional methods. These, in the context of crofting, have resulted in a land management system which contributes to conservation, and the crofter is now being recognised as a major element in the preservation of the landform and its unique characteristics.

There is another interesting aspect of the machair which has a cultural inference. In Ireland, the distribution of machair is linked to the Gaelic speaking areas (the Gaeltachta), which reflects the same situation in the Western Isles. Thus, it has been suggested that there could be devised a valid cultural definition of machair in parallel with its physical description.

The existence and nature of the machair has also made a significant contribution to the understanding of the various strata related to the human settlement in the islands. In its way, machair has provided a form of covering which contains a deep archaeological

Barra's airfield on the Traigh Mhor, used since 1936 as an airstrip

*Right: The sweeping curve of the white sand beach at Orosay,
near North Boisdale in South Uist*

QUALITY OF LIGHT

One aspect of the Southern Isles of which the visitor might not be immediately aware is the quality of the light. Dominated by the sea and sky, the canopy is all-embracing and offers the photographer, amateur or professional, unique opportunities to capture on film something of the atmospheric character of the islands, some of which is seen in the pictures in this book. Even on a day with clouds scudding in from the Atlantic, the ever-changing kaleidoscope of light presents an interesting challenge to the ability of the lens to freeze both time and space.

sequence, rising through the Bronze Age, Iron Age, Viking and medieval layers – all now being made accessible for assessment and interpretation as on-going 'digs' are progressed, at such sites as Udal in North Uist, at Rosinish in Benbecula, and at Dun Vulan in South Uist.

In sum, the island machairs encompass a wide range of interests which include the evolution of the landform, plants, birds and invertebrates, landscape, coastal scenery, archaeology and the history of human settlement. All of these are interrelated and have contributed to one of the unique physical assets of the Southern Isles.

If the sea has contributed to the complexity of the machair on the west coasts of the Southern Isles, it has also provided another range of prospects as viewed from landward. These are the off-shore islands, only the largest of which still carry populations, such as Berneray in the Sound of Harris, Grimsay, North Uist, Eriskay and Vatersay. But there are others which are now deserted, like those situated south of Barra: Sandray (uninhabited since 1931), Pabbay (deserted since 1911), Mingulay (deserted in 1912) and another Berneray, which was deserted by its population in 1891 with only lighthouse keepers living on the island until the Barra Head light (built in 1833) became automatic in the late 1970s.

View from Blashaval looking west over the moorland to Loch Fada

Opposite: Loch na Criege, North Uist. In the vicinity can be seen the remains of many Iron Age structures, such as duns or fortified dwellings

Added to these larger and once-inhabited islands are hundreds of others which have no resident community, but which at one time offered grazing for a few sheep or provided peat for fuel. One need only glance at the map of North Uist to appreciate the fantastic fretted seascape to the north of Lochmaddy and the sprinkling of islands around Barra.

Of particular interest are the Monach Isles which lie about five miles to the west of North Uist. Essentially they are little more than high sandbanks but supported a viable population until the late 1930s. Local tradition has it that before the sixteenth century, a massive five-mile stretch of sand, exposed at low water, connected the islands to North Uist, but then a huge tidal wave swept the sand bridge away to isolate the Monachs. Even so, the islands maintained a community, provided with a small post office and a school until some sixty years ago. The village can be seen through binoculars from the mainland of North Uist. A red brick lighthouse was built in 1864 but was discontinued in 1942. There are now plans to revitalise the building to serve as a sea-light for shipping using the western approaches of the Atlantic.

2 THE NATURAL HABITAT

View from Blashaval looking east to Lochmaddy and North Lee (2,693ft/821m)

Right: Mute swans enjoy the serenity on Loch Yeor, North Uist

WITH SOME 40 PER CENT of the total land area of the Western Isles now recognised as being of outstanding scenic value, it follows that the botany and zoology contained within the variety of island landscapes also have a particular significance. The combination of land, sea and inland water has produced habitats that support an astonishing variety of species, with the many offshore islands, now unpopulated or largely unvisited, adding to the kaleidoscopic character of the natural habitat. In recent years scientists have subjected many specific areas to detailed research, describing profiles which are then assessed and put forward for their recognition as Sites of Special Scientific Interest (SSSI). At times these designations create controversy, particularly if they involve crofting land and have a potential for

disturbing the natural development of crofting to achieve a better economic return for the effort which this system of land use entails.

On the other side of the coin, it is now accepted that the land management associated with crofting has made a significant contribution to the creation of natural habitats and environments which would not otherwise exist today had highly mechanised forms of farming been introduced. Indeed, it is *because* of the limitations of the available landforms in the islands, always open to exploitation, that these SSSIs attract the attention of visitors.

Of the forty Sites of Special Scientific Interest, most are less than 1,200 acres (500ha). One of the largest, 37,000 acres (15,000ha), is Loch an Duin in North Uist, with the South Uist machair, 15,000 acres (6,100ha), classed as being of outstanding significance. The Loch Druidibeg National Nature Reserve is of international importance because of its open freshwater system which has a wide range of trophic (concerned with nutrition) levels

which support communities of plants and animals. Its importance also stems from its coastal habitats of lagoon, dune and machair. The SSSIs at Balranald Bay and Loch nan Feithean include a reserve of national importance in the care of the Royal Society for the Protection of Birds.

The Monach Isles to the west of North Uist have been declared an area of national importance on account of the coastal habitats of calcareous dunes and machair. These are rich in flowers and provide an undisturbed pasture for barnacle geese feeding in the winter months. The islands are also a nursery for grey seals and form the largest breeding colony in Europe.

Because of the wide range of habitats, an equally wide variety of species of birds can be seen, including those which prefer the shelter provided by the few stands of trees in the Southern Isles, or by the scrub cover in places not accessible to deer or sheep. These can be seen at Ben Aulasary, Allt Volagair and Creagory in South Uist, and at Northbay and Brevig in Barra. These stands offer shelter for vagrants, blown off course by high winds. Islands in freshwater lochs often support a scrub cover of importance to birds.

The more mountainous areas of North and South Uist support golden eagles, a common sight from main roads at all times of the year, always on the hunt for small prey. At times, buzzards and merlins, hen harriers and short-eared owls may be caught out of the corner of the eye. A few kestrels inhabit the western parts of Benbecula and the Uists. On many of the freshwater lochs in the Uists and Barra the mute swan is a common sight. Loch Bee in South Uist in particular is noted for the hundreds of such birds which congregate on the shallow waters. The shallow machair lochs of the Uists and Benbecula are often crowded with a wide variety of ducks and waders – mallard, shovellers, teal, scaup, shelduck, widgeon and coot.

Around the cliffs and seashores, sea-birds abound, such as the herring gull, a determined scavenger, great and lesser black-backed gulls and black-headed gulls, which occur everywhere in very large numbers. Arctic skuas have in recent years established colonies in North Uist and Benbecula with some birds now moving farther south into South Uist.

A view of Ahmore Strand, near Truimsgarry, showing the tidal saltings. Close by is a loch with the remains of Dun Aonghais, dating from the Iron Age but occupied as late as c 1520. It is approached by a causeway which is now under water

The common silverweed thriving on the Machair Leathann, North Uist

The Animal Visitor Centre, North Uist, which has a wonderful number of exotic species on show. Here are llama and an African pygmy goat

That once-common bird throughout the British Isles, the corncrake, has found comparative refuge in the Western Isles, where the sympathetic system of crofting land management has allowed the species to enjoy life to the full. In summer months, the raucous calls of the bird can disturb one's sleep which is a small price to pay for the occasional sight of a corncrake scuttling for cover in the long grass.

Among the waders commonly seen are lapwing, dunlin, redshank, snipe and oystercatcher, the latter daintily treading the shorelands in search of food and tasty titbits.

To try and describe all the species of flora to be seen in the Southern Isles would take a chapter in itself. Suffice to say that the variety of landscapes in the islands offers the optimum conditions for plants to thrive in abundance. Coastal areas, dry and wet machair lands, shallow freshwater lochs, salt-marshes, hills and open moorland all have their own domestic flora. These include Hebridean orchids (with the fragrant orchid found only on Barra), sea thrift, sea rocket, silverweed, field gentian, moonwort, adder's tongue and white water lily, seen in peaty lochs. There are also many plants associated with Alpine habitats on the higher reaches of the islands.

Of the larger mammals, red deer occur in the Uists, but tend to be rather shy creatures. Otters live mainly on the coastal areas, and rabbits, because of their increasing numbers, are becoming more of a pest than an addition to the scenery. Grey seals often haul up on secluded beaches, particularly on the western shorelands of the islands. The slow-worm is the only reptile native to the Western Isles (it is really a legless lizard) and is often glimpsed basking in the sunshine in the summer months.

Added to these are freshwater fish (salmon, brown trout, sea trout and charr), some 600 species of beetle, 357 species of lepidoptera, a few butterflies, dragonflies, and the famous Hebridean bumblebee, so one can never say that these islands are lacking in variety.

LOCH DRUIDIBEG

THE LOCH DRUIDIBEG National Nature Reserve extends some 4,144 acres (1,677ha) and stretches across South Uist from the Atlantic coast to the Minch. It takes in a variety of habitats, including cultivated, fallow and uncultivated wet and dry areas, and coastal stretches. The Reserve was set up in 1958 with a deer fence erected for protection. Ten years later a number of native trees were planted, such as birch, hazel and alder, with the only group of now mature Scots pine to be found in the Uists. Three monkey puzzle trees add an interesting dimension. The plantation now provides food and shelter for small birds such as robin, greenfinch, thrush and blackbird. Cuckoos are often seen trying to muscle in on the nests of meadow pipits.

One of the few remaining native populations of greylag geese breed in

Early morning scenic colours looking over Lochs Hamasclett and Druidibeg, South Uist

the Reserve, to which are added others of the species in the winter-time. Offshore, many sea-birds can be seen most of the year, with migrants and vagrants. Small flocks of waders, sanderling and turnstones often feed along the tide line to the west.

The attempts to introduce rabbits, hedgehogs and ferrets (or domesticated polecats) have not been beneficial. The great numbers of rabbits populating the machair areas have reduced the grazing available for the domestic stock of the nearby crofting townships, and their burrowing has contributed to the erosion of the sandy ground. Ferrets, lost or released during rabbit trapping, are now a hazard for small mammals, birds and domestic fowl.

Hedgehogs, too, are now something of a problem. In 1974 seven animals were released into the wild in the hope that they would succumb to the climate. Instead they started to multiply and make their way north.

The headquarters of the RSPB Nature Reserve at Houghharry, North Uist. Houghharry is a good example of a traditional 'baile' or township. It is a nucleated settlement which was never cleared of its people, who continue to build on sites of their predecessors

They are now wreaking havoc on the machair, eating birds' eggs and threatening internationally important wader populations. The Royal Society for the Protection of Birds is currently preparing a planned offensive against the hedgehog which has badly hit bird numbers in the Uists. From the original seven animals released over twenty years ago, the population is now reckoned to be anything up to 10,000. On the mainland the animal is not a serious predator of birds' eggs. But the sheer numbers now scouring for food in the nesting areas of the island's flat western fringes has meant a high risk of the eggs being found before they have the chance to hatch. The breeding success of several species, including dunlin, redshank and snipe has been badly affected by the hogs.

In 1987 the Reserve was designated as a Site of Special Scientific Interest, and a year later it was recognised as part of the Uists' Environmentally Sensitive Area. Part of the Reserve is covered by two Geological Conservation Review Sites.

There is a self-guided walk around part of the Reserve, for which a leaflet is available locally. Access around the south-west corner of Loch Druidibeg is restricted during the bird breeding season (April to the end of August). Fishing on the lochs in the Reserve is by permit only.

The only RSPB Reserve to be found in the Western Isles (since 1966) is at Balranald, North Uist. Covering some 1,625 acres (658ha), the area takes in a variety of habitats, including the crofting township of Hougharry, itself of particular interest. At one time, the red-necked phalarope bred on the Reserve, but only single birds have been seen in recent years. The lochs and the fertile machairs are typical of those found in the islands and thus offer the living and breeding conditions which the birds prefer. While the emphasis is on birds at Balranald, the wide variety of habitats provides the flora and fauna of the area with an almost perfect environment in which to thrive.

The main loch within the Reserve is Loch nam Feithean, which has large areas of bog and is a favourite haunt of water fowl. A small offshore island, Causamul, serves as a breeding station for a number of Atlantic seals and supports the winter population of surface-feeding duck. During the summer months an RSPB warden is resident at Houghgarry. This crofting township is one of only a very few not to have suffered the experiences of the clearances of the last century. Its layout reflects the older nucleated settlement which was the common pattern during what is called the pre-crofting years, that is prior to the nineteenth century, and long before the crofting townships became linear in layout to follow the new straight roads which were built when the islands' hinterlands were being opened up.

3 THE PAST IN THE PRESENT

The solitary standing stone at Pollachar, South Uist, its probable date being the third millennium BC. It may have been used as a sea marker for prehistoric craft plying the coastal waters

LESS THAN TEN YEARS ago some archaeologists from Sheffield University were asked to have a look at a heap of what looked like scattered stones on a promontory on the west coast of South Uist. There was a clue in the name: Dun Vulan, which meant that at one time it had been a broch or galleried dun dating from the Iron Age, straddling the threshold from c 200BC to c AD200. Excavation work was begun and among the finds were small wooden tools. When the wood was examined it was found to be tamarack larch, a timber which grows in North America. In addition, the wood was found to contain holes made by the teredo mollusc which is found in warmer waters than are encountered off South Uist.

It seems likely that the original tree fell into the sea, or a river in Canada, two thousand years ago and was carried down the American coast

The remains of the chambered cairn below South Uneaval, North Uist. It dates from Neolithic times c 3000BC

Opposite: The standing stone at Beinn a' Charra, South Uist, probably dating to the third millennium BC. It is 17ft (5m) tall with commanding views of the coastal machair land

to the Caribbean and then into the Sargasso Sea for a number of years, to become infected by the mollusc. Finally, the wood was caught up in the Gulf Stream and found a resting place on the shores of South Uist, where it was put to good use by the Iron Age people of the island. This is only one of the many interesting facts which are coming to light as the ancient prehistoric remains of the Uists and Barra are being exposed by archaeological research to reveal the story of human habitation going back 4,000 years BC, if not earlier.

Exactly when the people of the New Stone Age (Neolithic) first appeared in the Western Isles will never be known. What is known is that the evidence for their existence is considerable, at least in the context of their monumental 'houses of the dead': those many-chambered cairns which litter the landscape. Their domestic settlements, however, are less in evidence, mainly because the construction materials used have left hardly anything which might have survived the passage of time.

For some reason North Uist seems to have been a favoured place for the Neolithic islanders, perhaps because of its proximity, just across the narrowest part of the Minch, to the Isle of Skye, where a number of chambered tombs are also located. In addition to some twenty chambered cairns, four settlement sites have been identified: Eilean Dhomhnaill at Loch Olabhat, and Udal, Eilean an Tighe and Carinish, all in North Uist. Only Alt Chrysal, on Barra, has revealed a settlement. It is significant, perhaps, that the North Uist sites are located on the western side of the island where, as today, the fertile machair land offered some potential for life and living for these early farmers, this allowing for the fact that the contemporary machair many thousands of years ago lay farther out into the now-submerged coast.

Radiocarbon dating of material unearthed from settlement hearth sites suggests a dating from 3300–2900BC. What this dating means is that the early Hebridean settlers were able to generate a formal social structure which, in time, enabled them to set their minds to building massive structures in stone: chambered cairns, solitary standing stones and stone circles. Many of these lithic monuments again tend to be concentrated in North Uist, with a tentative distribution of standing stones in South Uist.

This suggests that Neolithic society in the islands was sufficiently organised to have significant amounts of labour diverted from the routine

subsistence activities of farming, fishing and the collection of food. Of interest are the dozen or so stone axes recovered from island sites which are made from imported igneous material, porcellanite, found in Rathlin Island in County Antrim, Northern Ireland. These axes seemingly had a special status and were reserved for ritual rather than practical use, as they appear to have been deposited deliberately as votive offerings. Again, there is a suggestion of a level of sophistication, bordering on religious belief, which implies that island society, as elsewhere, was not as primitive as one might expect of people living over six thousand years ago.

A major icon of the New Stone Age is Barpa Langass in North Uist. Built around 3000BC it is a well-preserved passage grave situated on a hillside overlooking the present-day moorland, though it would have dominated a quite different landscape in its own time. Very few finds of significance have been discovered associated with the site, though pottery, charcoal and fragments of cremated human bones were removed by seekers of souvenirs who should have known better.

THE BRONZE AGE

OFFICIALLY THE NEOLITHIC PERIOD as such ended in Scotland around 2000BC with the appearance of metalworking settlers who introduced the Bronze Age. The transition, however, was not overnight and may have taken some centuries to become established. So far as the Western Isles were concerned, the New Age may have made its advent by the appearance on the horizon of one or two migrant craftsmen practising their new techniques and looking for patronage.

It is reckoned that the Bronze Age technology appeared in the islands around 1800BC, with the newcomers also importing a distinctive style of pottery and so becoming known as the 'Beaker People'. What is of particular interest is the heavy concentration of known settlements in the Western Isles, including the Isle of Skye, which is virtually unparalleled elsewhere in Europe. These settlements, which include Udal in North Uist, Rosinish, Benbecula and Alt Chrysal on Barra, are also associated with beaker burials, urn burials and unaccompanied burials in a spread from North Uist to Barra.

The Benbecula site at Rosinish has revealed that it dates from the second half of the second millennium BC. Quite a number of shards of beaker pottery have been found, including both crude vessels used for domestic purposes, and rather fine examples of the potter's craftsmanship, more than likely used in beaker burials.

In the context of its 'Age', the Bronze Age people in the Western Isles have not left much in the way of their metalwork, but that may be because what there is to be discovered still lies under peat deposits or under the sands of the machairs. The most celebrated find was in the north of Lewis,

The entrance to Barpa Langass, a Neolithic cairn which is one of the best preserved of its kind in North Uist. A good torch is needed to get an inside view

comprising a collection of tools, a socketed axe, a spearhead and fragments of a beaten bronze vessel. In the Southern Isles a bronze sword was uncovered in the peat bogs at Iochdar in South Uist. In 1991 a fishing boat crew, dredging for scallops on the sea bottom near the Shiant Isles, found a splendid gold torc in their nets. Dating from around 1000BC, it is the only one of its kind associated with the Western Isles.

The stone circle, Pobull Fhinn, near Langass, North Uist

THE IRON AGE

THE VARIOUS 'AGES' ARE of necessity convenient time slots to enable the various periods of occupation to be studied by the experts. No doubt there was some considerable overlapping, with the merging of one 'Age' into another as time moved towards the BC/AD threshold. Socio-economic and technical developments in, say, the Bronze Age undoubtedly advanced into the advent of what is called the Iron Age, from c 300BC to c AD200, though in the Western Isles the latter date can be extended for at least another two centuries as the buildings associated with the Iron Age continued to be occupied for domestic purposes at least.

In one particular, the Iron Age is represented by the Atlantic round-houses, among which are the broch towers, the most famous of which is that at Carloway, Lewis. However, there is plenty of evidence that these roundhouses were a common feature of the landscape of the Southern Isles. The term 'roundhouse' was adopted to encompass a wide variety of stone-built structures which included brochs, semi-brochs, galleried duns, island duns and other variants. The term also reflects a kind of unity in an architectural context which brings into close association the structures in the Western Isles and those in the Northern Isles of Orkney and Shetland. That same association suggests some kind of cultural bond between these island archipelagos.

There is still some question as to the function of these roundhouses – whether they were built as strongholds occupied by some local chief, were places of community refuge in times of trouble, or had some simple domestic purpose where the local community was small numerically.

On-going investigations on roundhouse sites in the Southern Isles reveal some peculiarities. The recent excavations at Dun Vulan on South Uist have revealed the presence of a substantial midden or refuse heap within the enclosure around the main structure, with the suggestion that it constituted some kind of status symbol and a demonstration of the affluence and power of the inhabitants. Again, the number of roundhouses located on Barra is far in excess of what might have been required by a fairly small island population, assuming that the roundhouses were restricted to the upper echelons of society (a case of too many chiefs and too few Indians). From the Barra example, it may well be that round-houses formed the standard unit of settlement throughout the Western Isles.

The general conclusion is that these structures were in the main the possessions of small communities, used as visible expressions of territorial markings. Even some of the small and now deserted islands south of Barra supported populations that imprinted their presence on the land by constructing their own roundhouses. On Barra the dozen or so sites are located on land less than 195ft (60m) above sea level – on the fertile machair in fact. Thus the presence of a roundhouse would seem to proclaim that the surrounding area was under some kind of community control; but that is a matter for conjecture.

Another particularly Hebridean expression in vernacular architectural terms associated with later centuries of the Iron Age is the wheelhouse. This type of construction is found widely in the Western Isles and in Shetland, but not on Skye or Orkney where intense archaeological activity over the past hundred years has not revealed the wheelhouse format. In essence, the wheelhouse is a semi-underground drystone construction with stone piers radiating from the central hub of the building, with much evidence indicating mastery of construction. Three outstanding examples

The ruined remains of a possible wheelhouse at Machair Leathann, on the northern coast of North Uist

in the Southern Isles can be seen at Sollas on North Uist, Kilpheder on South Uist and Clettravel on North Uist. It is arguable that the wheelhouse served the same basic functions as the roundhouse in that it highlighted the presence of an extended family group with territorial rights. They were certainly not defensive in nature and their existence may indicate settled social, if not political, conditions in the islands, something which would continue until the appearance of the Norsemen in the eighth century.

EARLY CHRISTIANITY IN THE ISLANDS

EXACTLY WHEN THE Christian Gospel arrived to make its impact on the peoples of the Western Isles is not known. A putative date is post-AD563 when the high-born Irish Christian monk, St Columba, landed on the island of Iona, off Mull, to set up a monastic school from which were sent itinerant monks charged with carrying the message of Christ to all and sundry, high and low.

There is no documentary record to indicate how these first missionaries were received by the island communities. There may have been initial language difficulties, assuming that the early clerics spoke only Irish or a

Below and overleaf: Trinity Temple at Carinish, North Uist, dating from the twelfth century. It fell into ruins, was reconstructed and then destroyed after the Reformation, c 1581. At one time in its early history it was a college of some importance. It was partly restored in the nineteenth century but was then allowed to deteriorate. Close by is Feith na Fala, the Field of Blood, where in 1601 a battle was fought between the MacLeods of Harris and the Uist MacDonalds

The medieval chapel and burial ground at Howmore, South Uist. In its time it was a monastery and college of some importance visited by scholars from Scotland and Europe. Four chapels can be seen, built of rubble and mortar. They were destroyed after the Scottish Reformation (1560)

Opposite: Detail of the walling of one of the medieval chapels at Howmore, South Uist

form of Gaelic. It is on record that when St Columba went to Skye, he could only gain converts through an interpreter, suggesting that the common language in the Hebrides was Pictish. In time the missionaries were able to make themselves understood and began to make converts. They also established their own religious centres, often crude huts but later made of stone from which the rites of Christianity were practised.

What is interesting is that the many religious sites associated with these early missionaries are still remembered. This indicates that the initial impacts made by them were sufficiently significant as to be absorbed by a folk memory, and later to be reinforced by a more permanent system of place-naming which survived the Norse occupation, emerging after the thirteenth century reasonably intact.

For instance, the name of the crofting township of Kildonnan, South Uist, may be an echo of former times when a religious cell or chapel once existed and was dedicated to St Donnan. He is more associated with the island of Eigg, where he and his followers were killed in AD617. A saint associated with Benbecula was Torranan who landed at the beach called Caligeo, near Ballivanich. Nearby he built a simple cell which he dedicated to St Columba, thus subsuming his personal missionary work on the island in favour of the inspiration he received from Columba to carry the Christian message to the Western Isles. At Balivanich today there are ruins of Teampull Chaluim Cille, though it post-dates St Torranan's times.

THE BENBECULA SYMBOL STONE

Long before the Scotti came from Ireland to colonise Argyll, what is now northern Scotland was ruled by the Picts. Apart from a number of place-names containing the element 'pit', the Picts have left only carved stones as a memory of their existence. These stones bore carved symbols, a crescent, fantastic animals, and images which look like mirrors and combs. The meaning of these symbols is still subject to investigation and interpretation.

Two Pictish stones have been found in the Southern Isles. One, with crude representations, was discovered on the island of Pabbay, south of Barra. The other was found at Strome Shunnamal in Benbecula, now lodged in the Museum in Edinburgh, and made from grey granite. The carved symbols are supposed to have been an indication of the presence of an important ruling class in the islands, with the stone being something of a totemic focal point for the Pictish society which once lived on Benbecula.

The only saint who has a specific territorial association is St Barr, whose name still survives at Cille Bharra on the island of Barra. This site is interesting because it is one of two in the Southern Isles which echo the structure and layout of a 'cashel', a collection of religious and secular buildings which made up a monastic community. The other cashel is at Howmore in South Uist. Most of these chapels are in a ruinous state today but are worth visiting if only to experience the atmosphere which exudes from former times.

THE VIKINGS

WHEN NORSEMEN STARTED to appear on the west coast of Scotland at the end of the seventh century, little did the inhabitants of the islands know that they were to become subject to a dominant rule that was to last for nearly 500 years. And yet the Vikings have left very little of archaeological substance to prove they were ever associated with the Western Isles. Apart from a handful of sites with Norse associations, there are virtually no monuments as such which can confidently be attributed to them. There is, however, place-name evidence to indicate that they were fairly widespread.

One interesting indication of the presence of the Norse in the Southern Isles can be seen at Cille Bharra. This is the replica of a rather unique stone discovered in 1865, the original now being in Edinburgh. It is a gravestone with a Celtic cross on one side and with Norse runes forming an inscription on the other. This runic stone proves with reasonable certainty that Cille Bharra was in continuous use as a place of Christian worship and a burial ground all throughout the Viking period.

The oldest place-names of Barra are almost entirely Norse in origin and most refer to the natural features of the island. A number of Viking graves have been discovered on the islands south of Barra and on nearby Eriskay which contain grave-goods left in the tomb for the use of the departed spirit.

SOME SITES TO VISIT

Teampull Chaluim Chille, North Uist (NF 873 765)
The site is in Clachan Shannda and is a very old religious place with the graveyard still in use. The dedication is to St Columba.

Teampull Chliamain, North Uist (NF 711 728)
This chapel site is located in the old graveyard north of Tigharry.

Teampull Chriosd, North Uist (NF 783 613)
Part of the west wall of the structure is still visible. Local tradition has it that it was built in the fourteenth century.

Teampull na Trianaid, North Uist (NF 816 603)
Though in a ruinous state, this is still an impressive structure dating from early in the thirteenth century, though it was repaired 150 years later. In medieval times it was well known as a university for priests, taught by a family of tutors, the MacVicars. One of the most famous students was the acclaimed fourteenth-century philosopher, Duns Scotus, who gained for himself a European reputation as a theologian. After the Reformation in 1560 the buildings fell into disrepair. Close by is Teampull Clann Mhic a' Phiocair, the burial ground for the MacVicars.

Teampull Chaluim Chille, Benbecula (NF 782 549)
This chapel is on raised ground close to Balivanich and is dedicated to St Columba. The walls are still fairly intact.

Teampull Mhuire, Benbecula (NF 765 537)
This chapel is at Nunton, in the old graveyard known as Cille Mhuire, in the area where a nunnery once existed, of which no remains are left. The stones of the nunnery were used to build a mansion for the island proprietor.

Teampull Clann a' Phiocair, at Carinish, North Uist, close by Trinity Temple. The Teampull belonged to the MacVicars who were for a couple of centuries the teachers at the college

The remains of the old chapel of Teampull Mhuire, Nunton, Benbecula, standing in the old graveyard dating from around the sixteenth century

Howmore, South Uist (NF 758 365)

This is a most important medieval church site, the origins of which may well go back to the earliest advent of Christianity in the islands. The main chapel could date from the eighth century and is reckoned to have been built on a levelled prehistoric site. The visible remains here are the ruins of two churches and three subsidiary chapels, one of which is a burial chapel for Clan Ranald. The original occupants provided legal, bardic, educational, musical and ecclesiastical services, mainly for the MacDonalds of Clanranald but no doubt for the locals as well.

Cille Bharra, Barra (NF 705 074)

Apart from the church at St Clement's at Rodel in South Harris, this religious complex is the most important of its kind in the Western Isles. As it stands today, the church was probably built around the twelfth century but may well be based on an older refurbished structure. The main church still has the north and south walls rising to about 8ft (2.5m) in places. To the east of the building are two chapels. St Mary's Chapel has been re-roofed to house the late-medieval carved tombstones which formerly lay in the graveyard. The burial ground contains the remains of many Barra folk, including those of the writer and novelist, Sir Compton MacKenzie.

Dun an Sticer, North Uist (NF 898 778)

A fairly well-preserved broch approached by three causeways which are just above water at low tide. There are the remains of later buildings – one inside the broch itself.

Dun Aonghais, North Uist (NF 856 738)

On an island in the loch, this is the Fort of Aonghus, Angus the Fair, who occupied it c 1520. It could be Iron Age or slightly later as it is of a more sophisticated design than many of the contemporary duns.

Above and right: St Barr's Church, part of the medieval complex of Cille Bharra, a settlement of religious buildings and associated secular quarters for the monks

Dun Scolpaig, North Uist (NF 731 751)
On an island in a loch, this was the site of a dun which was pulled down and replaced by a folly in 1830 by Dr Alexander MacLeod of Balelone.

Kilpheder Cross, North Uist (NF 726 745)
This cross (see left) stands on a hill to the right of the road. It was found in the churchyard and placed on its present site by Dr Alexander MacLeod who had a penchant for interfering with ancient remains.

Clettraval, North Uist (NF 749 713)
A chambered cairn and wheelhouse, the former dating from Neolithic times and the latter the fourth century.

Hougharry, North Uist (NF 705 710)
A good example of a traditional 'baile' or township. It is a nucleated settlement which has largely remained unchanged.

Teampull na Trionaid, North Uist (NF 818 605)
Probably dates from the twelfth century and was once a college of learning.

Barpa Langass, North Uist (NF 837 656)
A Neolithic passage grave and one of the best-preserved cairns in the Southern Isles.

Pobull Fhinn, North Uist (NF 843 365)
A fine stone circle called 'The People of Fion', on the south side of Beinn Langass. Oval in shape, at least twenty-four stones can be counted.

Teampull Chaluim Chille, Benbecula (NF 783 549)
A ruined chapel dedicated to St Columba.

Nunton House, Benbecula (NF 768 535)
A large house most of which is uninhabited, and the erstwhile home of the MacDonalds of Clanranald who owned Benbecula and South Uist. The family moved to Nunton House after their previous home, Ormacleit Castle in South Uist, was burnt down in 1715.

Borve Castle, Benbecula (NF 773 507)
Once at least three storeys high, the castle dates from the fourteenth century. It was still occupied in 1625. Local tradition has it that the castle was connected by an underground tunnel to Teampull Bhuigh, a church situated on the low hill about 500 yards to the south-west, now all but disappeared into the machair land.

Above: Scolpaig Tower, North Uist, resting on the site of an Iron Age dun pulled down in 1830 to be replaced by this folly. Scolpaig was the last rendezvous of smugglers in North Uist

Right: The remains of Borve Castle, Benbecula dating from the fourteenth century

Pollacharra, South Uist (NF 746 144)
A standing stone probably dating to the third millennium BC. It may be a sea marker for a prehistoric landing place.

Kilpheder Wheelhouse, South Uist (NF 735 205)
A wheelhouse perhaps dating from the second century.

Flora MacDonald's house, South Uist (NF 742 264)
This was not her birthplace but she lived for some time in this building. A cairn marks her association with the place.

Ormacleit Castle, South Uist (NF 738 318)
Once the home of the chief of Clanranald. It dates from 1701 and was burnt down in 1715.

Dun Vulan, South Uist (NF 715 298)
Site of a broch being excavated in detail to reveal its ancient secrets.

4 A PAINFUL HISTORY

FAR-TRAVELLED ISLANDERS

*In South Uist there is the story of
how a visitor from Japan was
waiting at a bus-stop close to a
filling station, near Howmore. As it
was raining, the garage owner
invited him into the building to
take shelter, in fluent Japanese.
Surprised at meeting someone who
could converse in his own language
he chatted with the owner and
settled down to wait for his bus.
Within a few minutes another
islander drove in to fill up his tank
with petrol. He commented on the
bad weather in perfect Japanese.
The amazement of the Japanese
visitor is not recorded but he left
South Uist with a great admiration
for the linguistic skills of the people
of the island. He did not know that,
within a matter of minutes, he had
encountered the only two people
who had spent many years in the
Far East.*

*Kismul Castle, Castlebay, Barra, with
the ferry* Lord of the Isles

DESPITE THE FACT THAT North Uist, Benbecula, South Uist and Barra are bound together by cultural and linguistic ties, similar community settlement characteristics, crofting land use and share some of the traumatic experiences of the last century at the height of the clearances, each island can lay claim to its own distinctive history, both secular and religious.

When Vikings appeared off the west coast of Scotland c AD800, their intent was plunder, no doubt attracted by stories of treasures contained in religious settlements and communities, with the island of Iona being the prime target. It was first raided in AD806, when many of the monks were murdered, and then revisited a number of times until the last raid in AD986. By then the Norsemen had converted to Christianity. Indeed, by the end of the thirteenth century the Bishop of Iona was ordained in Trondheim in Norway.

So far as the Western Isles were concerned there is plenty of place-name evidence that the islands, while hardly blessed with important religious centres, were attractive to the Vikings, if only as convenient and temporary bases for ongoing piratical raids into Ireland. By the advent of the ninth century, their interest in the islands was more centred on colonisation and settlement with their attention focused on the fresh prizes of Iceland, the Faroes and Greenland.

Their spread of settlement in the Western Isles is interesting, based on place-name evidence. In the north, some 99 of the 126 names of townships are of Norse origin with a further nine containing Norse elements. Lewis was the most densely populated, suggesting a cultural, if not physical, domination of the resident population. In the Southern Isles the density is more transparent with fewer Norse place-names. However, there are a number of sites in the Uists and Barra where graves and Viking pottery have been found. At the present time, two sites are of significance. One is at Drimore, South Uist, where a single house was excavated and found to be of the 'hall-type', common in the Norse world, and dated to the early tenth century. There are, however, some unanswered questions about the site. The other site is at Udal in North Uist. This is a more extensive Viking Age settlement where a series of buildings and Norse artefacts suggest a tenth-century occupation of a domestic nature.

In 1263 the Norse were defeated at the Battle of Largs and were persuaded to cede their territorial possessions to Scotland under the terms of

the Treaty of Perth in 1266. The Norse evacuation was not an overnight exercise. After some four centuries of Norse hegemony, it was inevitable that some vestigial elements of their political structures would remain to fill the vacuum – which is what happened, reflecting the situation in England after the Romans left in AD410, allowing existing Celtic chiefs to re-assert their former domination.

The departure of the Norse heralded the flowering of a new political entity, known as the Lordship of the Isles, which lasted until 1493, and began with John of Islay who was invested in 1354 as *Dominus Insularum*, 'Lord of the Isles'. His Gaelic title was *Ri Innse Gall*, 'King of the Hebrides', perhaps indicating that Gaelic, suppressed as a language during the Norse occupation, was coming into its own. Under the Lordship, clan or family surnames appeared in the Western Isles.

The Clans

IT IS LIKELY THAT the MacNeils of Barra, which island is mentioned in eleventh-century documents, had some connection with this insular territory. They received their overlordship from the Lord of the Isles, with their possession of the island dating from 1427 when Gill-Amhanain MacNeil obtained the title by charter from Alexander. After the dissolution of the Lordship, the MacNeil charter was confirmed by King James IV in 1495. The MacNeils were supreme masters of the sea and not above the occasional act of piracy. During the reign of King James VI, Ruairidh MacNeil seized an English vessel off the shores of Ireland. Queen Elizabeth complained to King James accusing him of piracy, which led to MacNeil being called to Edinburgh to answer for his conduct. He ignored the command and a ship was sent to arrest him.

Invited on board by trickery, he was hauled off to the Scottish capital to appear before the King who asked him why he had attacked a ship of a friendly nation. In reply, MacNeil said that he thought he was doing the King a service by injuring 'the woman who had murdered His Majesty's mother' (Mary Queen of Scots). He thus avoided a hanging but had his estate forfeited for a short time, after which he returned to Barra to ponder on his fortunate escape.

After Ruairidh came a continuous succession of six other chieftains which terminated with General Roderick MacNeil in 1827. Barra was sold to pay off the General's creditors in 1838, an event which heralded an unhappy time for the Barra islanders.

In 1937 Robert Lister MacNeil, Chief of Clan MacNeil, bought Kismul Castle in Castlebay and 12,000 acres (4,855ha) of Barra to become a landed proprietor in the country of his ancestors. He was descended from a branch of the MacNeils who had emigrated to Canada. He restored Kismul Castle to something of its former glory. He died in 1970 and is at rest in the

vault in the castle chapel. It is worth mentioning that the restoration of the castle was largely carried out by men from Barra, thus linking them with the original builders of Kismul Castle some 500 years previously.

Kismul Castle, Castlebay, Barra

In South Uist the dominant family was Clan Ranald who also had Benbecula in their possession. They were descended from Ranald, son of John, the first Lord of the Isles, who had the surname MacDonald. There were many branches of this family as one might expect from being connected to the powerful Lordship. When the Lordship was forfeited in 1493 and annexed to the Scottish Crown, the various chiefs were offered Crown Charters to confirm their landed possessions. Incidentally, the present heir apparent to the British throne, Prince Charles, has, among his other titles, that of Lord of the Isles.

In 1610 the Captain of Clanranald obtained a Charter in respect of lands in South Uist on payment of a feu duty which involved Clanranald maintaining a house and grounds and the provision of personal and military service for his superior. This provision of 'hunting and hosting' was a common feature of leases in the islands. Hosting was the organising of people for military service and their transport for military campaigns. The Captain found himself to be more than comfortable with this arrangement. In 1644 his income was reported to be £9,000, a fair sum in those days.

The fortunes of the Clanranald family in the Uists came to an untidy end in 1784, when the Chief was succeeded by a minor to the estates which paid £25,000 per annum and which had been in the father's possession for 500 years. By 1827, after thirty years devoted to high living in London and representing an English rotten borough in Parliament, he found himself on the verge of bankruptcy and his agents were obliged to wring every penny piece out of his estates.

In 1837 South Uist was sold for £84,229 to Lt-Col John Gordon of Cluny in Aberdeenshire. Two years later Benbecula was also sold to the same Colonel to sever the islands' connections with Clanranald.

In 1495 a royal Charter confirmed the title of the lands in North Uist to Hugh MacDonald of Sleat in Skye. This branch of the MacDonald family was one of the many which claimed descent from the Lordship of the Isles. Hugh died c 1498 and, according to local tradition, is buried in Sand in North Uist. Thereafter followed a short, turbulent period during which Hugh's sons (six in all and by as many mothers) claimed and counter-claimed rightful possession of the estates which included North Uist. After a period of relative stability the Sleat MacDonalds were able to settle down to enjoy their lands, that is until 1716 when, on account of the support offered by Sir John MacDonald to the Jacobite Earl of Mar, the estates were forfeited, and put up for sale in 1723. By means of a system of wheeling and dealing, the lands were bought for £21,000 by an Edinburgh lawyer acting on behalf of the Sleat family. A couple of years later the lawyer was able to enter into a contract of sale between himself and Sir Alexander MacDonald, a minor, who in 1727 received a Crown Charter of his lands 'erecting the whole into a Barony to be called the Barony of MacDonald'. In 1776 a descendant was created Baron MacDonald which meant in effect that the Sleat family never really lost control of their estates. However, North Uist was sold in 1855 to Sir James Powlett Ord, to break a MacDonald connection with the island which had lasted some five centuries.

The ruins of Ormacleit Castle, South Uist, the residence of the chief of Clanranald. It was built in 1707 and took seven years to complete, only to burn down in 1715. A French architect and masons were employed in its construction

The Turbulent Century

WHILE THE COMMON PEOPLE of the islands did not have an easy time of it during the centuries when the MacNeils and MacDonalds held sway, at least they knew how to live out their lives under the prevailing system. They lived in modest settlements and worked, not only to maintain their families but also to contribute to their land rentals. However, they did not have, by and large, security of tenure, unless they were part of the middle class who were able to negotiate legal agreements as to lease terms and levels of payments. Otherwise, the bulk of the population, who are seldom mentioned in historical documents, survived as best they could. They were normally housed in buildings made from perishable materials, like turf, which were regularly dismantled to provide manure for fields. Later, rough stone was used to build walls, with roofs being thatched. Essentially, the lower classes survived within the framework of a subsistence economy.

The introduction of the kelp industry (burning seaweed to make ash for industrial purposes) heralded a spell of relative comfort, though the work was hard and unpleasant, with most of the profits going to the landlord. In 1812, for instance, it was estimated that Lord MacDonald of Sleat, who owned North Uist, made £14,000 in that year alone. Kelp workers received a shilling a day, a fortune to them but a sum which hardly reflected an adequate recompense for their labour.

By the 1820s after the Peninsular War, prices for kelp began to fall, reflecting the introduction into Britain of foreign barilla. The problem was that during the three or four decades which saw the boom years of the kelp industry, the island populations had increased to such a level that over-crowding on the land was acute. About this time, the traditional landowners, in Barra and the Uists, began to sell off their estates to new owners who had no historical connection with their new possessions, with their agents failing to look at the small print in their sale contracts which mentioned the high levels of population with no visible means of support.

Because the Uists and Barra had been purchased as speculative investments, the new landlords, through their agents and factors, set about removing the main burdens on the estates – the people. Thus the nineteenth century was to be written on a page in island history dripping with cruelty, pain and inhumanity, conditions which the ordinary islander had no means of avoiding, legal or otherwise.

The Clearances

Barra

In 1851 a partial clearance took place in the island, when sixty-one destitute people made their slow way from Barra to Inverness. They sat down in front of the Town House there to see what the authorities could or would do for them. About forty people were sent to the parish poorhouse while the rest were given temporary lodgings. In the same year the *Quebec Times* had this to say in reporting on the situation in which emigrants from Barra and South Uist found themselves.

> We noticed in our last the deplorable condition of the 600 paupers who were sent to this country from the Kilrush Unions. We have today a still more dismal picture to draw. Many of our readers may not be aware that there lives such a personage as Colonel Gordon, proprietor of large estates, South Uist and Barra, in the highlands of Scotland. We are sorry to be obliged to introduce him to their notice under circumstances which will not give them a very favourable opinion of his character and heart. It appears the tenants of the above-mentioned estates were on the verge of starvation, and had probably become an eyesore to the gallant Colonel. He decided on shipping them to America.

South Uist

Between 1849 and 1851, upwards of 2,000 persons were forcibly shipped to Quebec. Some were induced to board the ships voluntarily under the promise that they would be conveyed free of all expense to Upper Canada where Government agents would give them work and grants of land. These promises were not fulfilled. The emigrants were turned adrift in Quebec and were compelled to beg their way to Upper Canada. The islanders' misfortunes were aggravated by the fact they could speak only Gaelic.

Prospective emigrants who refused to board the transports which Colonel Gordon had chartered for the clearance were hunted down with the aid of dogs, caught and bound, thrown onto the ships and despatched with no thought or concern for their condition. The suffering of the men, women and children who were the victims of these proceedings can only now be guessed at. However, there is a personal recollection from last century, noted down by a Catherine MacPhee from Iochdar in South Uist.

> I have seen the women putting the children in the carts which were being sent from Benbecula and the Iochdar to Loch Boisdale, while their husbands lay bound in the pens and were weeping beside them, without power to give them a helping hand, though the women themselves were crying aloud and their little children wailing to break their hearts. I have seen the big strong men, the champions of the countryside, the stalwarts of the world, being bound on Loch Boisdale quay and cast into the ship as would be done to a batch of horses or cattle in the boat, the bailiffs and the ground-officers and the constables and the police gathered behind them in pursuit of them. The God of life and He only knows all the loathsome work of men on that day.

NORTH UIST

Although the clearances of the people from the lands owned by General Gordon in Barra, South Uist and Benbecula were unrivalled in brutality, they were not unparalleled in their scope. Lord MacDonald's estate management in North Uist was solidly committed to the clearance ideal. Between 1849 and 1856 over 2,500 of the tenancy in the island were shipped over to Canada in the process of extensive removals and evictions. Crofting land left behind was added to existing farms with no qualms about the privations of those who had been browbeaten into accepting emigration as a solution to getting relief from a life of misery. No doubt those involved in the removals subscribed to the statement given by General Gordon who considered himself 'neither legally nor morally bound to support a population reduced to poverty by the will of Providence'.

A quiet resting place. The graveyard at Kilmuir, North Uist, which contains the memorial to Iain MacCodrum, the Uist bard, and memorials to the Clearances and to those islanders who died in Canada or the USA

THE STRUGGLE FOR LAND

WHEN THE BOTTOM FELL out of the market for kelp, a situation was created in which many estates found the overcrowding intolerable, with tenants unable to sustain themselves and their families with even the basic essentials for living. While the forced emigration of people was one solution, another spectre was to make an appearance on the scene which would focus attention on the dire lot of the tenantry as a whole, both in the Western Isles and throughout the Highland region. The spectre was famine, which had already cloaked Ireland with the results of the potato blight and was to extend its hands over the islands. In 1811 a report indicated that the potato constituted no less than four-fifths of the food of the crofter. A crop tolerant of lime deficiency and able to respond well to the use of seaweed, the potato was soon to become a staple diet, though it was resisted at first and not at all popular. But by the turn of the eighteenth century the crop was to be found everywhere.

The first outbreak of potato blight in Europe occurred in the summer of 1845. By the spring of 1846 all seemed well with the crop: by August it was devastated. As a contemporary observer noted:

> In the course of a week, frequently in the course of a single night or day, fields and patches of this vegetable, looking fair and flourishing, were blasted and withered and found to be unfit for human food.

By the end of 1846 it was estimated that at least three-quarters of the entire crofting population in the north-west Highlands and in the Western Isles was completely without food. A number of rescue agencies were created to alleviate the situation, which included Government, landlords and private charities. In the context of General Gordon's attitude to the tenantry on his island estates, the famine merely provided an opportunity to further harden his heart. One report on the plight of the people on Eriskay found 'greater wretchedness and privation' than on any other Highland property. On Barra the reporter found 'few families with any food at all'. Everything that could be eaten had been eaten, including the debilitating shellfish. Dysentery, typhoid and cholera were widespread.

Work programmes were started with payments made in quantities of meal, but not all crofters benefited from this alleviating measure. Lord MacDonald's factor on North Uist diverted a cargo of meal from Liverpool, intended to assist the tenantry, and resold it to make a 'handsome profit' for the estate. Out of a population of over 4,000, only 400 got work on a Government-funded drainage project. Only the fund-raising efforts of relief agencies averted the situation in Ireland, where tens of thousands died of starvation in ditches and roadsides, to litter the countryside with wasting corpses.

The War Memorial at Clachan-a-Luib, North Uist

Overleaf: A calm sunny morning in Lochmaddy, North Uist

Thus, what is seen today in the islands is a landscape of crofting communities and the product of well over a century of painful conflict to achieve the desire to possess a few acres of land.

The Kelp Industry

LIKE THE ALASKAN AND Californian gold rushes, the kelp industry in the Western Isles was a boom-and-bust affair. While it lasted it put hard cash into the pockets of estate tenants and made incredible fortunes for estate owners. When it failed it left a range of serious human problems which were only a foretaste of the miserable decades of the mid-nineteenth century yet to be experienced by the islanders.

The roots of the kelp industry go back to the early eighteenth century when it was realised that ash from burnt ferns, wood and seaweed was an important alkaline ingredient in the manufacture of glass and soap. The first kelp processed in Scotland was from Orkney, to be followed by the realisation that the Hebrides had a potential for making money from the large quantities of seaweed which were thrown up on the shores after Atlantic storms. The introduction of kelp burning into the North Uist economy started in 1735 when Hugh MacDonald of Baleshare island contracted with an Irishman (the Irish were familiar with the industry) to get the industry started. MacDonald reaped such huge profits that his example was not long ignored by other island proprietors. By 1785 many thousands of tons were being produced each year.

Two years later the burgeoning growth of the kelp industry was given a boost when duty on barilla (which, like kelp, produced alkali on burning) was increased which also raised the price per ton asked for kelp. The wars in Europe which restricted the import of barilla also placed a scarcity value on kelp. The main sources of kelp were North and South Uist and Barra, with the annual output from about 1764 to 1822 reaching some 800 tons. North Uist was the focal point for the industry; in 1812 the net proceeds from the island reached £14,000, with thousands of workers being employed in the peak months of June, July and August. To make one ton of kelp, twenty-four tons of seaweed were required.

The first documentary reference to kelp occurred in 1794 and relates to the industry in Barra.

Formerly the seaweed that grows upon the shore was used for manure; but since kelp has become so valuable, the proprietors everywhere have restricted the people of cutting it for that purpose, which is certainly prejudicial to agriculture… The tenants pay their rents by manufacturing kelp and sale of their cattle. The proprietor employs a number of them in making kelp upon his farm, for which he pays from £1 10s to £2 2s; and for the kelp made upon their own shores,

The Benbecula Mermaid

In the 1820s, near Griminish, Benbecula, a group of people cutting seaweed for fertiliser saw a creature described as 'a woman in miniature' thrashing about in the sea. A few days after, the dead body of the creature was washed up in Culla Bay. It was reported to have had an upper part the size of a well-developed four-year-old child, with long, dark, glossy hair. The lower part of the body was said to be like a salmon, but without scales. Many people came from the Uists to view the bizarre body. The factor of the Benbecula estate ordered a coffin and a shroud and the creature was given a decent burial on the shore of Culla Bay. What it was remains a mystery to this day. The fact that the estate factor thought the creature sufficiently humanoid to have it buried with some respect adds a fascinating twist to the story.

which he has at his disposal, £2 12s the ton, which is the highest manufacturing price given in the Highlands so far as I know. So that, from the sale of their cattle, and making of kelp, the people live very easy…

Even at these high production prices, the seller of the kelp could make up to £22 per ton, indicating the handsome returns made by the estates from free raw materials.

In 1817 the influence of the revived Spanish trade caused the Government to reduce the duty on imported salt and this seriously affected the kelp industry because salt could perform the same function as kelp ash. Then in 1822 the import duty on barilla was also reduced and the kelp industry fell into decline. By 1845 there was hardly any kelp-burning going on in the whole of the Western Highlands.

But that was not quite the end of the commercial interest in seaweed gathered in the islands. In 1883, a chemist, E. C. Stanford, discovered alginic acid which was to become an important ingredient in the food, textile, paper, pharmaceutical and cosmetic industries. This revived the interest in seaweed, and drying and milling plants were set up at Orosay, South Uist, and at Sponish, near Lochmaddy in North Uist about fifty years ago, with the seaweed being gathered by crofters to supplement their incomes.

Now mainly centred on South Uist, tangle or *laminaria* is gathered after it has been washed ashore by winter gales, or rockweed is collected, which is a year-round crop, giving part-time and casual employment to crofters. The weed is wind dried and sent for processing to plant on the Scottish mainland.

THE GAELIC HERITAGE

THE PEOPLE OF THE Uists and Barra have always remained true to their culture derived from the Gaelic language. During the last century the islands were a happy hunting ground for collectors such as John Francis Campbell of Islay, seeking out centuries-old folklore and folk-tales, with many of the latter now accorded international status. These collectors discovered men and women, unlettered in Gaelic but with amazing retentive memories, able to recite for hours on end, stories, genealogies of island families, historical events, folk tradition, medical lore, songs and poetry. These people were the Gaelic community's tradition-bearers who passed much of their knowledge on to succeeding generations. Though these people are much thinner on the ground now, some twentieth century storytellers have made a massive contribution to the recorded and documented Gaelic cultural heritage.

One was the late Angus MacMillan of Griminish on Benbecula. One collector over a period of eighteen months recorded from Angus some 5,000 large manuscript pages of stories. A further eighteen months of

A TASTE OF GAELIC

Each year in the Southern Isles, tourists can enjoy a glimpse of the Gaelic language and culture, should their visit coincide with the various festivals, arts and music events which have become established in the past few years. These include:

The Uist Mod (music competitions) in mid-June;
Lochmaddy Boat Festival in mid-June;
Ceolas Music School (musical workshops and informal entertainment) on South Uist, beginning of July;
Feis Bharraigh (multi-arts festival) in early July;
Feis Tir an Eorna (music festival on North Uist), early to mid-July;
Barra Highland Games at Borve from early to mid-July;
Berneray Week in mid-July;
Feis Tir a Mhurain (music festival), Lionacleit, Benbecula, in early August.
For those with an outdoor bent there is the Twin Peaks Hill Race on North Uist in early August.

The Barra Museum at Craigston, Barra

recording produced the same amount of material for the School of Scottish Studies. Some of the longer tales could take over seven hours in the telling. Angus was unable to read or write, but his prodigious memory was sufficient for him to become something of a record in the field of international folklore studies. He died in 1954.

On Barra, the late John MacPherson from Northbay contributed many stories to the treasure chest of Gaelic heritage on the island. On South Uist, Angus MacLellan of Loch Eynort was a story-teller of consummate ability, the product of an immemorial tradition that is better preserved and more cultivated in the Western Isles than anywhere else in Western Europe. Another South Uist man, Duncan MacDonald, from the township of Peninerine, was from the same stock, being well versed in the traditional oral Gaelic culture and belief.

These tradition-bearers were not isolated members of their island communities but were representative of a long-standing pride in their cultural heritage. They followed in the footsteps of the island fore-runners. One came of the family of MacMhuirich (modern Currie) who lived in Stilligary in South Uist. The family were the bards to Clanranald dating back to the sixteenth century and kept commonplace books in which items of clan history, anecdotes, genealogy, elegies and panegyrics for their own and other chiefs were entered, all written in classical Gaelic. In fact the

MacMhuirichs were the last practitioners of Gaelic bardic verse anywhere. Though not a native of Benbecula but descended from a notable island family, Alexander MacDonald (Alasdair Mac Mhaighstir Alasdair), was the most famous Gaelic poet of the eighteenth century. His longest work, a description of a voyage by the galley of Clanranald, *Blessing of the Ship*, has been described as the finest sea-poem ever written in Britain (see page 76).

Interior of the thatched cottage museum at Craigston, showing a reconstructed croft house

THE HERITAGE MOVEMENT

THROUGHOUT THE WESTERN ISLES, and particularly during the past decade or so, a number of historical societies have been set up, all dedicated to ensuring that local traditions, culture and aspects of local history are being preserved for future generations. Many of these *Commuinn Eachdraidh* have their own premises where artefacts, photographs and documents are on display, including detailed genealogical information readily available to anyone seeking information about family roots. These centres are: Barra Heritage Centre, Castlebay, Craigston (Barra Museum); Kildonnan Museum, South Uist; Sgoil Lionacleit (Liniclate School), on Benbecula; and Taigh Chearsabhaigh at Lochmaddy, North Uist.

Opposite: Details of some internal and external wall decoration at the Catholic Church at Garrynamonie, South Uist. The smallest picture depicts Our Lady of Sorrows

RELIGION

CHRISTIANITY WAS INTRODUCED TO the islands during the sixth and seventh centuries by monks from the island of Iona, emanating from the religious centre set up by St Columba in AD563. During the ensuing centuries the Catholic religion gradually became debased until 1651 when Clanranald appealed from South Uist to the Congregation of Propaganda in Rome for priests. Eventually St Vincent de Paul, the founder of the Lazarites, provided missionary help in the form of three priests, including one Father Duggan who, over a five-year period, reconciled islanders from Benbecula to Barra Head to the Catholic faith. He is still remembered by a pass over the Barra hills, Bealach a' Dhugain.

By 1671 the Hebridean mission was placed under the care of Blessed Oliver Plunket, the Archbishop of Armagh in Northern Ireland (martyred in 1679), and the faith was consolidated. However, both Clanranald in South Uist and MacNeil in Barra then abandoned their faith, and the Catholic population was sorely persecuted. Clanranald used to drive his tenants to the Protestant Church with a thin yellow cane, to try to compel them to follow the 'religion of the yellow stick'. Failure to attend the church meant instant eviction from their homes. Matters came to a head when a MacDonald of Glenaladale in Inverness-shire on the mainland, who had interested himself in the plight of the South Uist people, bought an estate in Prince Edward Island, Canada, and emigrated there with 200 persons from South Uist to practise their beliefs in a free environment.

The year 1829 saw the Roman Catholic Relief Act, since when Barra and South Uist have been served by a succession of Catholic priests. Today, both Protestants and Catholics in Barra, Eriskay, South Uist and Benbecula live together on the best of terms. North Uist is almost wholly Protestant.

Main Street, Castlebay, Barra, with the Catholic Church, 'Our Lady, Star of the Sea'

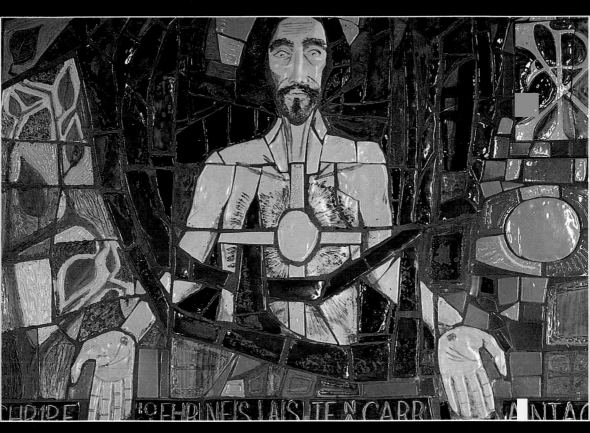

5 ISLAND CAPITALS AND SMALL ISLANDS

WITHIN THE EGALITARIAN CROFTING communities on each of the main Southern Isles of the Hebridean chain, each small township is equal to any other. However, history and geography have a say in which township or settlement emerges to become a focal point for an island, to become the effective capital for the community. Lochmaddy, Balivanich, Lochboisdale and Castlebay fall into this category even though, in their respective islands, there are much larger townships which could claim to be the 'capital'.

LOCHMADDY

THE MAIN TOWNSHIP OF North Uist first appeared in documentary records in 1616, in connection with a complaint concerning piracy and murder in the more northerly island of Lewis which makes mention of 'Lochmadie on the coast of Uist' as being a rendezvous for pirates. Later, in the 1630s, Lochmaddy became a centre for a commercial herring fishery, set up by Charles I in an effort to make a profit from the rich fishing grounds in the waters of the Minch. But his scheme did not last and by 1695 Lochmaddy went into decline. However, an echo of that prosperous time can still be appreciated in that the present Taigh Chearsabhaigh stands on the site of Taigh an t-Salainn (The Salt House) built in the 1630s to provide salt for the herring industry. The footings of this building were still visible in 1741 when Taigh Chearsabhaigh was erected on the site, to become one of the first buildings in North Uist to have a slated roof.

During the eighteenth and nineteenth centuries, Taigh Chearsabhaigh was used as an inn until 1864 when the Lochmaddy Hotel was built to offer a more sophisticated service to the growing number of visitors to the island. By the 1950s the building was beginning to suffer from its old age and, while used for boat repairs, might have come to a sad end. However, the North Uist Historical Society and the Uist Art Association got together to lease the building from North Uist Estates and began a programme of reconstruction. The result, opened in 1995, is a new and significant focal

Peace and calm in Lochmaddy harbour

LOCHMADDY MARKET – 1903

Just outside Lochmaddy is Cnoc na Feile, Market Stance. Fairs were held here in July and September for the sale of cattle and horses; according to tradition these may date back to the early 1600s. After the fairs were over the estate factors held rent collections to receive cash for overdue payments. The following describes the scene in 1903:

'From an early hour on the market day the whole locality is astir. Everyone who desires to buy or sell, meet friends, or have a day of merriment, is on the move and all the highways and byways to the market stance present unwonted activity. Old women are driven in carts, while the young women, dressed in holiday attire, walk on foot, usually accompanied by some of their male friends. Men residing at a distance use ponies – shaggy animals with long switching tails. The whisky tent is in working order from the arrival of the first customer. The vendor of confections and the dealer in cheap jewellery and cheap pictures are much in evidence and usually succeed in carrying out a fair amount of business. By the forenoon the market is in full swing and a picturesque picture is presented – men and women of all ages and attired in all manner of dress, from the simple home-made blue kelt or hodden grey to the latest and most striking fineries from the mainland.'

Opposite: Stained-glass window in Lochmaddy Church of Scotland, opened in 1911

point for the island's heritage and artistic displays.

In 1799 a Report on the North Uist Estate and its potential for development suggested that the erection of a few houses would be the ideal way to start a new settlement which would become the focal point for administrative, commercial and industrial activity. Within a few years, the new township was enjoying the trappings of success. By 1827 the main block of the Old Court House had been built and two years later the Estate factor took charge of the post office. The importance of Lochmaddy came in 1843 when it gained 'Post Town' status. Then came the start of the boom years of the Minch herring industry (1870) which necessitated the installation of a telegraph office (1872) and the opening of a branch of the Caledonian Bank (1873). In 1875 a new Sheriff Court House was completed, with the old Court building used as a prison until 1891.

Recognition of the increasing importance of Lochmaddy as a centre for the whole of the Southern Isles came in the 1880s with a resident Procurator Fiscal, a resident solicitor, the appointment of the first professional postmaster, and the harbour being established as a port of call for steamers from Glasgow and Dunvegan in Skye. The school, built in 1877, was attracting more pupils and the efforts to establish a hospital came to fruition in 1884. By the turn of the century, Lochmaddy had all the trappings of an administrative centre. The start of another herring boom in the 1920s, which lasted for a decade, provided a welcome boost to the commercial activities of the town.

Lochmaddy today exudes an honest pride in the way in which it has grown over the past two centuries: slowly and in response to the needs of the island population. It is a town of humane dimensions; even the traffic is well behaved, though when the ferry arrives there is the time-honoured buzz of excitement and activity which is characteristic of any island town worthy of the title 'capital'.

BALIVANICH

THE IMPORTANCE OF BALIVANICH to the whole of the Uists has yet to be assessed in social terms. The town has been described as a vortex, a kind of magnet which has attracted a wide range of services and activities which have resulted in Balivanich becoming quite uncharacteristic of any other township in the Southern Isles. Yet there are surviving traces of its origins, which go back some 1,500 years. The ruin of Teampull Chaluim Chille (St Columba's temple) lies in a boggy marsh and is seldom visited. The later monastery which gave Balivanich its name, Baile na Mhanich, the town of the monks, has completely disappeared. Local tradition has, however, not quite forgotten the very considerable religious associations which this locale has had over many centuries.

The recent history of Balivanich started with the establishment of an

The Birlinn of Clanranald

(see page 69)

'The sun bursting golden-yellow,
*   out of his husk,*
The sky grew wild and hot-
*   breathing,*
Unsheathing a fell tusk,
Then turned wave-blue, thick,
*   dun-bellied,*
Fierce and forbidding,
Every hue that would be in a plaid
In it kneading.
Now they hoisted the speckled sails
Peaked and close-wrought,
And stretched out the stubborn
*   shrouds*
Tough and taut
To the long-resined shafts
Of the mast.
With adroit and firm-drawn
*   knotting*
These were made fast
Through the eyes of the hooks and
*   rings;*
Swiftly and expertly
Each rope put right of the rigging;
And orderly
The men took up their stations and
*   were ready.'*

airport during World War II, as a key location in Britain's North Atlantic coastal defences. Its strategic significance continues today with the permanent RAF presence. When the Army Rocket Testing facilities were set up in South Uist in 1957, Balivanich and its future were set on a course which has proceeded apace. In addition, the causeway and bridge connections between North Uist (1942) and South Uist (1963) almost dictated that the township would become a focal centre for the Southern Isles, which it certainly is today.

The extensive rather sprawling military housing, together with Local Authority estates, give the place an impression of bustle. This, coupled with the many commercial and Local Authority administrative facilities delegated from Stornoway in Lewis, gives a rather unexpected contrast to the more familiar crofting townships of the islands.

From an economic viewpoint, Balivanich is an undoubted plus for the Southern Isles, though some argue that by the concentration of too many activities and facilities, Balivanich will expand to the detriment of other nodal points desperate to survive. Only time will tell whether Balivanich will serve as an example of *modus operandi* to be followed in other parts of the Southern Isles.

LOCHBOISDALE

THIS TOWNSHIP WAS FIRST settled by people who were removed from their lands on the west side of South Uist after the island was purchased by Colonel Gordon of Cluny in 1838. Thus Lochboisdale does not have the same claim to a long historic lineage as do Lochmaddy and Castlebay. Even so, its position at the head of Loch Boisdale was to provide the incentive for significant growth derived from the herring industry boom of last century and the increasing use of its piers by steamers bringing visitors into South Uist.

The township received some recognition in 1881 when a post office was established, which later became a telegraph office to cater for the business activity based on herring. However, it was not until fifty-eight years later, in 1939, that Lochboisdale was recorded in the Post Office 'List of Telephone Exchanges'.

At the present time, it is a port of call for the car ferry from Oban, which also services Castlebay in Barra, and as such is an important terminus. The layout of Lochboisdale is quite informal and its appearance in general has changed little over the years, though it is much smarter due to recent improvements which have done away with the former 'quaintness' of some of the older buildings. The hotel, bank, post office and tourist office are focal points for the township, which in 1998 has a population of around 300.

CASTLEBAY

WITH ITS LARGE NATURAL and sheltered harbour, Castlebay has no doubt been a settlement at least since the building of Kismul Castle in the fifteenth century. The township came into its own in 1869 when a leading herring curer, James Methuen, decided to use Castlebay as a herring port, setting up facilities for handling the huge catches of fish. Within a few years it rivalled other Hebridean herring ports like Lochboisdale and Stornoway. It is on record that there were occasions when Castlebay's spacious harbour could not accommodate all the boats which required berths to unload their catches. In 1886 up to 400 fishing boats fished out of Castlebay, and during the height of the season, May to June, some 2,000 people were employed to cope with the landings.

Around the shores of the bay were temporary huts and bothies, known as fishing stations, where girls gutted and salted the herring and packed them into whitewood barrels destined for European destinations such as St Petersburg, Danzig, Hamburg and Stettin. During World War I trade declined and when hostilities ceased the industry took some time to

The car ferry Lord of the Isles *leaving Lochboisdale, South Uist*

Overleaf: A calm scene at Castlebay, Barra

ISLAND BULBS

In 1956 a scheme was promoted to investigate the suitability of using fertile machair land for the growing of daffodil and tulip bulbs. Ten years later the scheme was proved to be a success and it was foreseen that large-scale and concentrated bulb-growing in the islands could be a useful economic activity for crofters. A Dutch firm was commissioned to investigate the possibility of reclaiming an area of some 1,500 acres (607ha) of the tidal calcareous sands at Valley Strand in North Uist. But the idea never came to fruition, being turned down by the Scottish Office.

But the idea did not die. In 1996, six sites in the Western Isles were identified for a new experiment, three of these being at Milton in South Uist, Tigharry in North Uist and one on the island of Berneray. Planting areas were prepared and fenced off. The bulbs thrived, with twenty-six of the forty suggested species being identified for further trials. With the continuing drive to diversify croft production, the islands may well become a 'Little Holland' with bulb fields adding their colourful contribution to the scenic delights on the coastal machair land.

recover. When it did, Castlebay continued to enjoy something of its former prosperity until the outbreak of World War II. Again Castlebay managed to buck the trend of decline and was recognised as a fishing port for another twenty years or so. When a ban on herring fishing was imposed due to declining stocks, Castlebay turned to white fish and shellfish, which has kept some semblance of a fishing fleet and industry reasonably well rewarded.

Present-day Castlebay is an attractive township amply provided with all the usual facilities and services. The new community school – a distinctive modern building on the edge of the township – contains a library, swimming pool and sports hall and is the venue of many social and community events. During the annual Feis Bharraigh, which runs for two weeks in early July, the whole island comes alive, with visitors and islanders alike taking part in competitive and leisure events all based on the culture and language of the Gael.

THE SMALLER ISLANDS

LIVING ON SMALL ISLANDS in the Hebrides has always been fraught with difficulty: access to social and public services, higher cost of living, transport problems and lack of gainful and satisfying employment. While island communities a century ago tended to accept these difficulties as normal, nowadays there are higher expectations, some of which materialise only after many years of campaigning for a standard of living equivalent to that enjoyed by urban and more structured rural communities.

It was in 1861 that a Census Report first offered a definition of an island: '… any piece of solid land surrounded by water, which affords sufficient vegetation to support one or more sheep, or which is inhabited by man'. A number of smaller islands in the Outer Hebridean chain once supported small but socially significant populations but are now deserted to become derelict, useless hulks lying like anchored flotsam in fertile seas. Others still are on the brink of enjoying a new status, being integrated into a larger socio-economic framework. At the time of writing, Scalpay Island, off Harris, was given a fixed-link (bridge, in common parlance) in 1997. A causeway is being developed to link North Uist with the island of Berneray in the Sound of Harris. And Vatersay has been linked by causeway to Barra. Only Eriskay, of the still-populated islands in the Western Isles, awaits the attention of the political administrator for a solution to its current problems.

BERNERAY

ALTHOUGH BERNERAY IN THE Sound of Harris lies closer to North Uist, it is officially part of the Parish of Harris. All the population lives on the south-east side, the western coast of the island (2,496 acres/1,010ha) being occupied by low-lying machair, rough grazing and sand dunes. The two crofting townships, Borve and Ruisgarry, maintain a current population of about 141 (1991 Census). The highest number occurred in 1841 (713 dwelling in 130 houses) due to an influx of people cleared from the nearby island of Pabbay and the Harris Estate. In the 1850s some people were also cleared from the island, after which the population declined from 524 in 1901 to the present number.

Berneray is served by a small but good harbour funded in the 1980s by European Community money as part of the plans of the Western Isles Council to improve infrastructure within the islands. It is served from Leverburgh in Harris and Otternish in North Uist. A causeway, recently completed, provides a reliable solid link with North Uist.

The island economy is based on crofting, sheep-farming and fishing, the latter mainly prawns, lobsters and velvet crabs. The community maintains a justified pride in the island, often manifested in viable ideas to improve the standard of housing and living. A number of new houses recently built on Berneray is an outward sign of confidence and determination to keep the island's future bright.

ERISKAY

WITH A CURRENT POPULATION of 179 (1991 Census), Eriskay still waits for a causeway link between its main landing harbour at Haun and Ludac in South Uist. The wait may be a long one because one of the conditions in the provision of a causeway financed by European money is that the island has to demonstrate a potential for what the politicians call 'economic outflow'. With the once-flourishing fishing industry now a shadow of its former self, and Eriskay fishermen forced to land on South Uist or Barra, that condition may never be realised. The result of uncertainty about the island's future is a slow decline of not only the adult population but the school population – by any island standard, the hope for the future.

Eriskay is certainly not fertile. Its base of Archaean gneiss is overlain with peat. In 1838 a number of crofters threatened with eviction from South Uist settled on the island, even though it was reckoned to be so poor that sheep could hardly survive. But they set to work to make 'lazybeds' by fertilising peat with seaweed in raised platforms to grow barley, oats and potatoes for sustenance and survival. By 1841 some eighty people (living in twelve houses) managed to gain a foothold and establish the island's community, looking to the sea for their economic future.

In time Eriskay was to become one of the most important herring fishing centres on Scotland's west coast. The islanders' success in the prosecution of the fishing led to a hefty population increase – to 466 in 1881, a figure which remained stable until the 1930s. Thereafter a decline set in which now threatens to continue unless some practical links are provided between the island and South Uist.

THE ERISKAY PONY

In the late 1970s, the native breed of Eriskay pony nearly became extinct. Only the existence of an entire 100 per cent Eriskay stallion, called Eric, averted a crisis. Since then the breed has been built up from twenty mares, with Eric's help, and now has an optimistic future. The Eriskay pony is a small (12 hands high), docile, intelligent animal which is descended from a race of wild horses which roamed the forests of the Highlands in prehistoric times. It is said that the 'little grey palfrey' ridden by King Robert the Bruce at the Battle of Bannockburn in 1314 was of the same stock.

The Eriskay pony has thus escaped extinction through cross-breeding and there are now many genuine ponies used as working and riding animals on many of the islands. In the recent past the pony was used on crofts for carrying peat, hay, crops and seaweed from the shore for manuring the land and harrowing fields. A society for the preservation of the Eriskay pony ensures that the breed will continue into the future. Contact the Secretary at St Michael's Church, Eriskay.

The altar of St Michael's of the Sea, Eriskay, opened in 1903 but since renovated. The unique altar-piece is the bow of a lifeboat from HMS Hermes, *washed overboard while the ship was engaged in exercises off St Kilda. It came ashore at Pollachar in a damaged condition but the bow section was sufficiently intact to be used for this unique purpose. Reminiscent of the pulpit in Melville's* Moby Dick, *it is eminently fitting for an island church*

Opposite: The beach on the west side of Eriskay

Overleaf: The multicoloured machair on Eriskay

The present population is scattered among a number of small townships stretching from the north of the island to Acairseid in the mid-south, lying at the head of an inlet which cuts deep into the island and is the best anchorage for Eriskay. The two main hills, Ben Scrien (609ft/186m) and Ben Stack (403ft/123m) are a geological continuation southwards of the hilly eastern belt of South Uist.

Despite its setbacks, the Eriskay community still displays an air of confidence and determination to continue its existence into the far future. The facilities at Haun (Norse: havn, a haven) provide the basic necessities with its well-stocked village store, a good primary school with some thirty pupils, a post office and a pub called Am Politician, named after the ship which went ashore in 1941 laden with 20,000 cases of whisky destined for the American market. The incident provided writer Sir Compton MacKenzie with the plot for the still-popular film *Whisky Galore*.

The Roman Catholic Church at Haun was opened in 1903. Its altar-piece is the bow of a lifeboat washed ashore from HMS *Hermes* and the

THE *ANNIE JANE*

In September 1853 the emigrant ship Annie Jane *was wrecked on the island of Vatersay. She left Liverpool for America with a cargo of 385 'redemptioners', a term given to emigrants who booked passages that were to be paid for by instalments out of their earnings after they arrived on the other side of the Atlantic.*

Because of stormy weather the ship had to return to Liverpool twice but made a third and final attempt. The weather, however, worsened and the Annie Jane *was blown northwards towards the Western Isles and, in particular, the west side of the island of Vatersay. Just before midnight on Wednesday 28 September 1853 she struck rocks and the foremast toppled, going through the side of the ship, which ended up broadside against the force of the waves. By two o'clock the* Annie Jane *had broken up into three sections with hundreds of men, women and children dead in the water and on the beach. The total number lost in the tragedy was 333. Of the emigrants, only sixty survived.*

A granite monument to the dead overlooks Bagh Siar on Vatersay and is well worth a visit, if only to reflect in silence the circumstances of the loss of the Annie Jane *and her passengers.*

church bell is a ship's bell recovered from the German battleship *Derflinger*, sunk at Scapa Flow. Both these items reinforce Eriskay's longstanding association with the sea.

Access to Eriskay is by a small car ferry running weekdays between Ludac, in South Uist, and Haun. A passenger ferry runs from Ludac to Eoligarry on Barra across the Sound of Barra, a thirty-five minute journey.

VATERSAY

If the level of the sea ever rises significantly, Vatersay could become two islands. At the present time the two parts are joined by a low isthmus of sandy hillocks with a bay on each side of it. The island is connected to neighbouring Barra by a causeway completed in 1990 which allows the islanders access to the services, facilities and social delights at Castlebay.

Vatersay has been inhabited for many centuries. The current population is seventy-two (1991 Census). This figure compares with some 240 people recorded for the year 1931 and demonstrates the fragile socio-economic framework in which many island communities live. At the turn of the century Vatersay was an island farm. At the same time many landless cottars (or squatters) on Barra, itself overcrowded, were agitating for room to move, to live and make a living. In 1901 the Government, under what it chose to call 'excessive pressure', bought 3,000 acres (1,214ha) in Barra to relieve the situation and create new land holdings. But this move, while welcomed, left many dissatisfied with their situation. In 1902 several cottars applied to the Congested Districts Board for ground on Vatersay for planting potatoes. Some 60 acres (24ha) at Uidh on Vatersay were purchased and divided among fifty-one cottars, who planted seed potatoes but failed to produce satisfactory crops.

Over the next four years matters slowly came to a head until 1907 when six cottars from Barra and the nearby island of Mingulay decided to stake their claim to land on Vatersay and went into crofting history as the 'Vatersay Raiders'. Attempts to remove them failed and they were arrested and sent to Edinburgh for trial. Each was sentenced to six months' imprisonment. But the point had been made. The raiders became public heroes and were given early release. By 1909 Vatersay had been purchased by the Congested Districts Board and the island community recognised as bona fide crofters.

But for many years the comparative isolation of Vatersay dictated conditions which saw the loss of some 140 people between 1931 and 1961. The construction of the causeway has helped to stabilise the present community now dependent on crofting (sheep and cattle) and fishing.

MINGULAY

The last of the population of this island, south of Barra, left in 1912. Mingulay is now a sad and lonely memorial to the process of island

desertion. Yet it has had a history of occupation going back some two thousand years through the Norse era and possibly to the Iron Age.

At the turn of the century Mingulay had a population of 140, a community of islanders who wrested a subsistence living from their land, some thirty families living in houses, the remains of which can still be seen and are still in a surprising state of preservation. The Chapel house, called St Columba's Chapel, was built in 1898 and included a beautiful altar which is now a side altar in Our Lady Star of the Sea Church at Castlebay, Barra. The schoolhouse, built in 1881, is now roofless but it is an indication that the Mingulay community was, a century ago, in reasonably good heart to have made this provision.

Most of the population of Mingulay moved to Vatersay between 1908 and 1911, by which time only six families were left and it became impossible for them to survive in isolation. They finally moved away in 1912 to leave their island township as a kind of icon of the nineteenth century.

Access to the island is difficult, even in summer months; the Barra Tourist Office will have information for intending visitors.

Prince Charlie's Bay on Eriskay. It was here that Bonnie Prince Charlie landed on 23 July 1745, his first step on Scottish soil. Less than a year later, after his defeat at the Battle of Culloden in April 1746, the Prince was in the Uists trying to escape to France and freedom

Overleaf: The Vatersay island isthmus with Bagh Siar and Vatersay Bay

6 FAMOUS NAMES

THE DUKE OF TARANTO

France and South Uist are linked together through the Duke of Taranto. His name was Jacques Etienne Joseph Alexandre MacDonald and he was one of Napoleon's marshals. His father, who lived at Howmore in South Uist, was named Neil MacEachan but he changed his name to MacDonald. A staunch Jacobite, he was forced to flee to France with Bonnie Prince Charlie after the latter's defeat at the Battle of Culloden in April 1746. His son, the future Duke, was born at Sedan.

The Duke's military abilities caught the attention of Napoleon and he rose through the ranks to be ennobled among the élite of France. In 1826 the Duke paid a visit to Howmore to see his father's birthplace. Before returning to France he took a box of ancestral South Uist soil which was buried with him in his grave at Courcelles-le-Roi.

THERE ARE TWO CLASSES of 'famous names' associated with the Southern Isles. There are those who have come in from the outside to make their mark on the social and cultural scene and make a useful contribution to the overall life of the islands. And there are others, native-born, who have made an impact both locally and abroad on the pages of history, demonstrating that islands are not always closed communities but have the ability to rise above the idea of relative isolation which is too often common currency, even today.

SIR COMPTON MACKENZIE

One of the most successful British films of all time was *Whisky Galore*. Based on the grounding in 1941 of the 12,000-tonne cargo ship *Politician* off Eriskay, the plot was used by Compton MacKenzie, first for a book and then for a film script. The film, made in 1947, was a hilarious take-off of the frenzied and cunning attempts by islanders in the Uists and Barra to remove from the wreck cases of whisky intended for the American market. For their efforts, some men were arrested and appeared before the Sheriff at Lochmaddy; sentences imposed were imprisonment for up to two months. The wreck of the *Politician* was later cut in two, with the forepart being towed to Rothesay for scrap and the aft end being left under the waters of Eriskay Sound.

Another film based on a book by MacKenzie was *Rockets Galore* which highlighted the advent of the Army Rocket Range in South Uist in the 1950s.

Though Compton MacKenzie was quintessentially English, he became a passionate advocate of Scottish determination. In 1931 he was elected as Scottish Nationalist Rector of Glasgow University. During World War I he served in the Dardanelles before becoming Head of British Intelligence in the Aegean sector. After that he embarked on a very successful writing career before he decided to make Barra his home. The house he built in 1935 is a large white bungalow which overlooks the cockle strand which also serves as the island airstrip. It was bought in the late 1990s by MacKenzie's great nephew, the actor Alan Howard.

During the 1930s Compton MacKenzie and his friend, John Lorne Campbell of the island of Canna in the Inner Hebrides, set up the Sea League.

This was concerned with providing the fishermen of the Western Isles with an articulate voice, protesting against illegal trawling in Minch waters, and particularly within the then nationally recognised three-mile limit. While the Sea League had some success it was up against the trawling interests of Hull, Grimsby and Fleetwood who had the ear of people in high places to ensure that the League's attempts to stop trawling did not get very far.

It was not until 1964 that the Fishery Limits Act was passed, long after serious damage had been done to the Minch fishing grounds by illegal trawling and indiscriminate dredging of the sea bottom which destroyed spawning beds to the extent that the Minch waters now contain only a shadow of previous fishing wealth.

MacKenzie first visited Barra in 1928 and lived on the island from 1935 to 1945. He died, ironically for a Scottish Nationalist, on 30 November 1972 – St Andrew's Day. His funeral on Barra was dramatic and might well have been scripted by himself. His body was flown to the island and taken to Eoligarry cemetery to the sound of the pipes played by his long-standing friend Calum Johnston. Immediately after Sir Compton's interment, Calum died of a heart attack, to be buried at Eoligarry two days later.

FLORA MacDONALD

Flora MacDonald's name might never have been known in the context of Highland history had it not been for the attempt of Bonnie Prince Charlie to try and win the British throne for his father. As a fugitive on the run after the ill-fated Battle of Culloden in April 1746, the Prince found himself on South Uist with some companions, all at a loss as to how to escape and gain freedom to France. An unsuccessful attempt to charter a vessel at Stornoway, Lewis, left them no alternative but to make their slow way into the Southern Isles to find some temporary refuge at Coradale on the east side of South Uist.

It was luck more than anything else that put Flora MacDonald in the right place at the right time, when she was contacted and asked for her assistance to help the Prince escape. At first she was reluctant, but then agreed even though she realised she was placing herself and her family in great danger. After a series of narrow escapes from parties of Government forces on the island, she arranged for Bonnie Prince Charlie to be dressed up as a woman servant, Betty Burke, and sail over the sea to Skye and into Highland history.

Danger from capture by the English soldiers on Skye was no less than it had been in the Uists, but the Prince managed to elude them and make his way farther south, eventually to embark on a French vessel on 20 September 1746, some five months after his defeat at Culloden. Flora MacDonald was arrested in July at Portree in Skye for the part she played in helping the Prince to escape.

MacLEODS V MacDONALDS

At Carinish, North Uist, close by Trinity Temple is Feith na Fala, the Field of Blood. This was the site of the Battle of Carinish, which took place in 1601 and is reputedly the last battle to be fought in Scotland solely with swords, and bows and arrows.

The opposing forces were the MacDonalds of Sleat, in Skye, and the MacLeods of Harris and the conflict was the result of an ongoing feud which reached boiling point when Donald MacDonald divorced his wife, Mary MacLeod, offending the MacLeods and sending Mary home humiliated. Sixty Skye MacLeods sailed across the Minch to North Uist and arrived at Trinity Temple to wreak revenge. They were met by sixteen MacDonalds who literally chopped the MacLeods to pieces, with only two of the latter managing to escape. A third, Donald Glas MacLeod attempted to escape but was caught and, according to oral tradition, was hit on the head and killed.

He was subsequently buried at Trinity Temple. In 1840 a skull with a deep gash in it was reported 'lying about in the church', thus lending weight to one detail of the story. All the other dead MacLeods were buried were they fell at Cnoc Mhic Dhomhuil Ghlais (Hillock of Donald Glas), beside the shore.

The house on South Uist, where she lived for some time, is still seen at Milton. The low ruined walls surround a tall, slender cairn erected by the Clan MacDonald. At her trial in London she gave a good account of herself and her actions and was released, her exploits having captured the popular imagination. She later went to Carolina in the United States, but eventually returned to Scotland. In 1773 she met Dr Samuel Johnson, then touring the highlands with his companion, James Boswell. Johnson wrote of her, 'She is a little woman of genteel appearance, mighty soft and well bred... Her name will be mentioned in history, and, if courage and fidelity be virtues, mentioned with honour'.

REVEREND JAMES MACDONALD

Before John MacDonald, 19th Chief of Clanranald, died in 1794, he arranged that his eldest son, Ranald George, be tutored by a native of Uist, James MacDonald, who was also to be the lad's travelling companion when he was old enough to undertake the obligatory Grand Tour of Europe. James MacDonald was born in 1772 at Paible, North Uist, proud possessor of a long island lineage of a family which had once ruled the island. Thus he had the right background for the task which Clanranald desired for his eldest son. What he did not know was that James MacDonald was to become famous in his own right, both in his own country and in Europe.

James MacDonald, after receiving a licence to preach from Edinburgh University, went to Germany, initially to learn German, but was soon noted for his fluency in French, Spanish, Italian, Swedish and Danish. Through influential connections he found himself at the Court at Weimar and freely mixed with some of the prominent German philosophers of the day.

After returning to Scotland, MacDonald became a minister at Anstruther in Fife, but only for a short time. He was soon off for an extended visit to Sweden with his charge, the young Ranald George, the 20th Chief of Clanranald. In that country, the young lad created a scandal with his dubious liaison with the wife of a merchant operating in Stockholm, for which MacDonald was blamed, though he managed to extricate himself with some difficulty. He had not realised that the young Clanranald, even before he had come of age, had amassed debts of £47,000, all a burden on the Uist estate and which was eventually to see North Uist pass out of the Clanranald possession.

In his busy life, MacDonald managed to visit his native heath in the Western Isles to write his main work, *General View of the Agriculture of the Hebrides*, hailed as the best book on the subject ever written. He died

Flora MacDonald's memorial cairn at Milton, South Uist. Though she was not born here, she lived for a while in the house, now ruined. It was she who helped the fugitive Bonnie Prince Charlie to escape to Skye after crossing the Minch. The prince was disguised as Betty Burke

AN EARLY ISLAND PHOTOGRAPHER

In 1881 Archibald Chisholm arrived in North Uist to act as Her Majesty's Procurator Fiscal, and as Crown Prosecutor of those who had transgressed the law. Much of the litigation brought to the Sheriff Court House in Lochmaddy was run of the mill, until the passing of the Crofters Act in 1886 at which time the Court had to deal with many cases involving disputes over rents. These rents were imposed on crofters by the North Uist Estate, owned by Sir John Orde, who from the outset had objected vigorously to the Act's provisions which included the asking of fair rents for land.

Mr Chisolm was a popular and well-respected figure in the islands from Uist to Barra, so much so that he generated a hot resentment from Sir John. Matters came to a head between the two men when Chisholm was served with a 'Notice to Remove' from the property he had rented since 1882. This was an unheard-of situation: the representative of the Crown being effectively evicted from his home. Chisholm was even refused lodging in the Lochmaddy Hotel, which was owned by the Estate.

Part of the problem was that Chisholm was a competent amateur photographer who, in his travels from North Uist to Barra, always carried his heavy, brass-bound mahogany half-plate field camera and tripod around with him to record life in the islands. Some of his photographs depict evictions
(continued opposite)

in 1810, aged thirty-eight, leaving an estate of a mere £16, the fall-out from the disastrous break in a highly promising career when he took the young Clanranald to Sweden. It is a matter for conjecture whether MacDonald, an established authority on Hebridean agriculture, might have introduced a decisive influence for good into the economic development of his native islands.

FATHER ALLAN MACDONALD

In 1884 Father Allan MacDonald arrived at Lochboisdale, South Uist, to take over the Parish of Daliburgh which also included the island of Eriskay. At that time it was a very poor charge, with his parishioners living on the very margin of existence. It was also the period during which crofters were making their views known to the members of the Napier Commission, set up to look into the conditions of crofters and cottars in the Highlands and Islands. In addition, over 80 per cent of the population were practising Catholics, yet the schools were run by non-Catholics and by non-Gaelic speakers.

Despite these difficulties Father MacDonald, through patience and perseverance, managed to introduce an environment of tolerance and respect into his parish work. It was he who suggested that a hospital be built at Daliburgh, the same facility which exists today and known as Bute Hospital. He also worked to get a new church built on Eriskay, opened in May 1903 and paid for by funds subscribed by both Catholics and non-Catholics who had been inspired by his work in the islands. A sum of £200 was paid over by the Eriskay fishermen who had decided to devote the proceeds of one night's fishing, which, as it happened, turned out to be a record catch.

He is mainly remembered today for his work in gathering traditional Gaelic folklore, amounting to what is probably the greatest collection ever made by one person of material connected with one definite locality. Much of this collection has been published through the efforts of the late John Lorne Campbell of Canna, one of the pre-eminent Gaelic scholars of this century.

Father Allan MacDonald died, aged forty-six, in October 1905, as the result of a severe cold which developed into acute pneumonia. Medical help was slow in coming to his aid, because at that time there was only one doctor to serve the whole of Uist and Eriskay. Almost a century later Father Allan still has a place in the folk memory of the islanders of Eriskay.

ANGUS MACASKILL

The island of Berneray, in the western approaches of the Sound of Harris, is famous for one of its sons, Angus MacAskill, popularly known in his day as the 'Berneray Giant'. Born on the island near Shiabhagh in 1825, he emigrated to Cape Breton in Canada. He grew to become one of the world's 'healthy' giants, that is one whose height was not the result of disease. At his peak he was 7ft 9in (2.15m) tall and weighed in at just over 30 stones (193kg). He was noted for his ability to lift large boulders against all comers. He died in 1863, aged thirty-eight years. His association with Berneray is now commemorated with a cairn erected a few years ago near the place of his birth.

SIR NORMAN MACLEOD

Visitors to Berneray may be surprised to know of a connection between the island and the Battle of Worcester (1651). To the north of the island, close by Sand Hill, is the oldest building on Berneray, known as the Gunnery of MacLeod. Above the lintel is a marble slab bearing a Latin inscription which tells us that Sir Norman MacLeod of Berneray, a 'distinguished knight', was born here in 1614. He was proprietor of the island and was, in his time, a respected scholar and patron of the arts.

When King Charles I tried to impose episcopacy on the independent Church of Scotland he was met with opposition. The situation was partially resolved by his signing of the National Covenant in 1638 and the establishment of a short-lived Presbyterian system of church government. Then civil war broke out in England, with Oliver Cromwell finding himself in the ascendant and backed by his well-disciplined Ironsides. He consolidated his position by disposing of Parliament and leaving in its place a ridiculous and insolent 'Rump'. In 1649 Charles I was brought to trial and executed at Whitehall. The monarchy was restored eleven years later, in 1660, though this hardly brought any peace to the country.

In the Highlands, many chiefs, most of whom were Royalists, watched the unfolding events with some justifiable concern, including Norman MacLeod of Berneray. Their reaction was to move south with the Royal army making its way through Scotland and crossing the border into England. It is documented that 'one Macloud-herris hath brought up a regiment from the furthest Highlands who had, for the most part, bare pieces of rough skins on their feet for shoes'.

By the time the Royalists reached Worcester they had a force of 12,000 men who were shortly to face the 30,000-strong Cromwell army. The battle was fierce with little quarter given on either side. Norman MacLeod of Berneray was knighted on the field for his bravery. The cost to the MacLeod contingent was heavy, however, it being virtually wiped out.

After the battle MacLeod was captured and taken to the Tower of London where he was imprisoned for eighteen months until he escaped in 1653 to return to his native island. He was to live until 1705, dying at the age of ninety-one. He is buried at St Clement's Church at Rodel in Harris, leaving a considerable mark in the folk memory of Berneray as a gentleman, a warrior, a respecter of Gaelic tradition and one whose home was open to all.

(continued)
in the Lochmaddy area. And who better to know about the exact day, time and place of proposed evictions than the Procurator Fiscal, so that the events could be recorded? No doubt this was one of the irritating aspects which created dissension between Chisholm and Sir John Orde.

Eventually Chisolm was able to gain access to Ostrom House, near Lochmaddy, as his recognised residence. A number of years ago his original photographic plates were found in the attic of the old Lochmaddy bank house, less than 100 yards (483km) from Ostrom. These are now preserved for posterity. Many of Chisholm's photos (some shown here) were reproduced as postcards showing life in the islands around 1900.

Chisholm's views of Kentangval and the Post Office, Eriskay

7 OUT AND ABOUT

I N RECENT YEARS the Western Isles Tourist Board has been aware of the fact that many visitors to the Southern Isles relish the chance to leave the car and take to the moors, hills and shorelands. In response to many requests for the best and safest routes and walks which offer plenty of interest, the Board has produced a series of cheap pamphlets which detail walks of moderate category. These allow visitors to 'home in' on the detail in a small area, including highlights of wildlife, historic and prehistoric sites and something of the geological make-up of the islands. In addition, other recommended walks, none of which are partic-

THE CROFTING CODE

In the islands there is a Crofting Code to be followed. Many areas are in the nature of working ground for crofters, even on the open moorland and hills. The following 'ground' rules have been devised in the interest of all who use the countryside:

- *Avoid damaging crops in the growing season in the crofting townships.*
- *Never leave gates open, to avoid the possibility of livestock wandering.*
- *Keep dogs under control at all times and on a leash, particularly where livestock may be near at hand.*
- *Cars should be parked where they will not cause a problem for others.*
- *Respect both historical and ancient monuments; they are the visible heritage of the islands.*
- *Protect wildlife and plants, particularly breeding birds.*

require the comprehensive information to enjoy their visit, the OS Landranger Series is recommended. There are other types of map available, produced by the Western Isles Tourist Board, which highlight historic and prehistoric sites, information points and visitor facilities. These are particularly useful because they are bilingual (Gaelic and English) and assist anyone who might, by chance, misread a signpost.

ACCESS

IN GENERAL MOST OF the Southern Isles can be accessed by the public but there are times in the year when estates indulge in shooting over the ground. At these times it is recommended that the visitor obtain local information to find out what restrictions might be in force. In addition, it should be realised that open moorland and hills constitute the 'factory floor' of crofters, over which livestock, particularly sheep, tend to wander at will. Visitors seeking the delights of Loch Druidibeg Nature Reserve should seek advice before entering into areas where birds could be disturbed during the breeding months.

WEATHER AND WALKS

THE WEATHER IN THE ISLANDS can be changeable. In general, the months of May and June tend to be the sunniest, with reasonably dry weather being the norm between May and August. On most days in the islands there is some wind, coming off the Atlantic, which can introduce a chill factor but it is not unpleasant and is usually countered by warm sunshine. Prevailing winds in the islands tend to be south-westerly. Early mornings in the summer months can produce dead calm conditions when one can feel at peace with the world. Be advised though that when in the higher hills the weather can change quickly and often without warning.

If taking advantage of some of the recommended walks, which never exceed the 'moderate' category, suitable clothing and footwear should be worn. For instance, due to the non-draining nature of the moorland, the ground can become very boggy after wet weather. All of the Western Isles walks guides have miniature maps with the north compass bearing, so that a compass becomes a useful piece of kit in the unlikely event of losing one's bearings.

And it goes without saying that information should be left with someone on any route to be taken, with an estimated time of return. If such a person is not available and you leave your car parked, a visible note of the walk details should be left on the dashboard. All these are sensible precautions and help to make any visit to the islands pleasurable and memorable.

ularly arduous, are contained in June Parker's *Walks in the Western Isles* (see Further Reading page 109). There are thirteen walks listed, from the island of Berneray in the Sound of Harris, to the island of Vatersay, with North Uist, Benbecula, South Uist, Eriskay and Barra in between.

The Tourist Board recommended walks include the circuit round the Lochmaddy area; discovering the chambered cairn at Barpa Langass on North Uist; Loch Druidibeg in South Uist; the cockleshell strand at Eoligarry to the north of Barra; and a visit to the island of Vatersay. None of these walks exceeds four hours. The associated pamphlets include detailed maps.

While discovering the Southern Isles, maps can be a useful source of information. For those who require pin-point detail, the Ordnance Survey Pathfinder Series (1:25000) will provide all that is needed for the visitor to home in on a particular locality. For those who need less detail but still

Vatersay Bay with the island of Sandray beyond

View from Crogary na Hoe, North Uist, over the South Harris hills

Useful Information and Places to Visit

Tourist Information Centres

Tourist Offices
26 Cromwell Street, Stornoway, Lewis HS1 2DD
Tel: 01851 703088   Fax: 01851 705244
Open all year

Pier Road, Lochmaddy, North Uist
Tel: 01876 500321
Open early April to mid-October.

Pier Road, Lochboisdale, South Uist
Tel: 01878 700286 Open early April to mid-October.

Main Street, Castlebay, Isle of Barra
Tel: 01871 810336 www.witb.co.uk
Open early April to mid-October.

Air Links

British Regional Airways
Benbecula Airport, Isle of Benbecula, HS7 5LW
Tel: 01870 602310

Barra Airport
Northbay, Isle of Barra, PA80 5XD

Ferry Services

Caledonian MacBrayne
Head Office:
The Ferry Terminal, Gourock, PA19 1QP
Tel: 01475 650100   Fax: 01475 650268

Local offices:
Lochmaddy, North Uist
Tel: 01876 500337   Fax: 01876 500412
Lochboisdale, South Uist
Tel: 01878 700288   Fax: 01878 700635
Castlebay, Barra
Tel: 01871 810306   Fax: 01871 810627

PLACES TO VISIT

Taigh Chearsabhagh
Lochmaddy, North Uist. Tel: 01876 500293
www.taigh-chearsabhagh.org
Museum and arts centre.

Left: The car ferry Hebridean Isles
Below: Kilmuir church, North Uist, built in 1894
Overleaf: Castlebay, Barra

Balranald Nature Reserve
North Uist, www.rspb.org.uk/reserves/balranald
RSPB bird reserve: resident warden during
the summer.

Loch Druidibeg National Nature Reserve
One of the largest breeding grounds in Britain for
the greylag goose. A permit can be obtained from the
warden at Grogarry Lodge.

Dun an Sticer
Newton Ferry, North Uist
Dun last occupied in 1602.

Barpa Langass, North Uist
5,000 year-old chambered cairn, off the A867.

Teampull na Trionaid, Carinish, North Uist
Ruined medieval ecclesiastical site dating c. 1200.

Sgoil Lionacleit, Benbecula
Tel: 01870 602864   Tel: 01870 603539 (Sports centre)
www.cne-siar.gov.uk/school/lionacleit/
Community school with museum and sports facilities;
all open to the public.

Borve Castle, Benbecula
Impressive ruined walls of medieval castle.

Nunton Church, near Aird, Benbecula
On the B892, dating from mid-fourteenth century.

Benbecula Gold Club, 39 Winfield Way, Balivanich,
Benbecula, HS7 5LH
Tel: 01870 603275
www.benbeculagolfclub.co.uk
A 9-hole course where visitors are welcome.

Our Lady of the Isles, on Ben Rueval, South Uist
Erected in 1957 by the local community, close by the
A865.

Howmore, South Uist
Ancient chapels from the fourteenth century, off the A865
road. The burial ground of Clanranald.

Ormacleit Castle, South Uist
Early ruined eighteenth century castle, off the A865.

Kildonan Museum, Kildonan, South Uist
Tel: 01878 710343
Recently renovated museum with local history displays
and tea-rooms.

Flora MacDonald's House, Milton, South Uist
Ruined building and memorial cairn, off A865 road.

Askernish Golf Course, Askernish, South Uist
Tel: 01878 700083
www.askernishgolfcourse.com
Just off the A865, with views across the Atlantic and
the Machair.

Standing Stone, Pollachar, South Uist
Impressive monolith at the end of the B888 road with
views across the Sound of Barra.

Cille, Bharra, Barra
Thirteenth-century religious settlement, with restored
church.

Kisimul Castle, Castle Bay, Barra
Fifteenth-century castle on an island in the bay. Open
to the public.

Castlebay Community School, Castlebay. Barra
Tel: 01871 810471
Has a swimming pool, library and sports hall.

Barra Heritage Centre, Castlebay, Barra
Tel: 01871 810413   email: info@barraheritage.com
www.barraheritage.com
Local history exhibitions, restaurant and cultural activities.

Craigston Museum, Craigston, Barra
A thatched cottage museum with local history display.

Annie Jane Monument, Vatersay Island
The memorial to the loss of the vessel Annie Jane in 1853.

Lochmaddy Boat Festival, Lochmaddy, North Uist
Boat festival in May of June each year.

Feis Bharraigh (Barra Fest), Castlebay, Barra
Tel: 01871 810088
www. www.barrafest.co.uk
Music and arts festival held in July.

Feis Tir an Eorna, Paible, North Uist
Cultural events lasting one week in mid-July.

North Uist Highland Games, Hosta, North Uist
Local competitive events in mid-July

South Uist Highland Games, Askernish, South Uist
Local competitive events late in July.

Feis Tir a Mhurain, Lioncleit, Benbecula
Music and Gaelic arts festival in early August.

Uist Animal Visitor Centre, Bayhead, North Uist
Domestic and exotic breeds of animals.

Eriskay
6-hole golf course. Eriskay ponies can be seen.

PLACE-NAMES AND THEIR MEANINGS

COMPARED WITH THE VERY high density of place-names in Lewis and Harris derived from the Norse occupation of the Western Isles, from c AD800, the number of such names in the Southern Isles is considerably less. What one can make of this fact is a matter for conjecture and speculation. Most likely it is a reflection that Lewis in particular was the main base for the Vikings with the islands to the south serving as stop-overs for parties on their way to and from the rich pickings in Ireland and along the west coast of Scotland. There were, of course, a number of more permanent settlements, established after the Norse reduced their raiding forays in favour of colonisation. Typically, many of the Norse-derived place-names are associated with coastal features and prominent land features seen from the sea, such as high hills and mountains. Offshore island names are almost certainly of Norse origin, as one might well expect, for they were sure markers for vessels sailing seawards and in need of signs that they were on the correct course.

While many of these Norse-derived place-names have survived the passing of centuries, many others are pure Gaelic or are Gaelicised – the result of native Gaelic speakers, particularly on coastal fringes, naming features which were important to them as they ferried themselves across water or needed sea marks when out fishing. The Sound of Harris is an example of this kind of naming, with the many rocks, skerries, shoals and small islands and islets scattering this stretch of water from the Atlantic to the Minch. The word skerry is itself derived from the Norse 'sker' meaning a rock in the sea.

The present-day 'Uist' has appeared in early documents in a number of forms: Ivist, Ywyst, Huyst, Eusta, West and Ust and this short list is not exhaustive. 'Ivist' appears in early Norse sagas and might refer to an in-dwelling or habitation. But a case can be argued for other meanings, presenting the etymologist with a hard nut to crack.

The Gaelic for Benbecula is Beinn na Faoghla, the mountain of the fords, a name which recalls the times a few decades ago when a crossing could be made between North and South Uist by travelling over the tidal sands into and out of Benbecula. The only 'mountain' on Benbecula is Rueval which stands a mere 407ft (124m) above sea-level on the north side of the island. Like Uist, the island's name appears in a number of forms: Vynvawle (1372), Beanbeacla (1449), Beandmoyll (1535) and Benvalgha (1549), among others. Even trying to find some common phonetic element seems an impossible task, though the prefix of the double-element name might well centre on Rueval as a bare rounded hill (Gaelic: *maol*, meaning bald or bare).

The Gaelic name for Barra is Barraidh, supposedly derived from the Norse for Barr's Island, which could

External wall decoration of St Barr's Church, Northbay, Barra. The figure, a mosaic made entirely from sea shells, is of St Barr (c AD550–623) after whom the island is named. The church was built in 1906

be acceptable if, by the time the Norse appeared in the Western Isles c AD800, they found the island closely associated with St Barr, who was a Celtic saint of the seventh century. The Norse contribution to the original name was the addition of the suffix 'ey' (island). However, the Norse were pagans until AD1000 and they might not have sustained the found name of an island based on a Christian saint. If they had a different name for Barra it seems to have been lost.

It was, however, a different situation with islands called Pabbay (Priest's Isle). On these lonely locations, solitary hermits or anchorites made their cells for the purpose of meditation. They had extremely simple huts which offered a basic shelter from the elements, not worth the attention of the Norse, and were thus left alone but recorded as a sea marker.

Of the three island 'capitals', Castlebay on Barra is the odd one out, being purely English, though Gaelic speakers refer to it as Bagh a' Chasteil. Lochboisdale in South Uist presents a problem, though the 'loch' element is easily understood. In a document of c 1400, the place-name is 'Boysdale', while in 1549 the name appears as 'Vayhastil' and 'Baghastill', both indicating the presence of a castle or its remains. This castle is actually on the small island of Calvay, at the entrance to the present Loch Boisdale. Lochboisdale, if one excludes the 'loch', is the Bay of the Castle.

The entrance to Lochmaddy in North Uist is guarded by three basaltic rocks, called the Maddies, or dogs, hence Loch nam Madadh, a name which has an easy transference from Gaelic to English.

The following is a list of Norse place-name elements which will give the visitor an indication of how a particular name came into being, with reasonable certainty.

Nes	a headland	eg, Carinish (Kari's Ness), North Uist
ey	an island	eg, Eriskay (Eric's Isle)
borg	a fort	eg, Dalabrog (the dale of the fort), South Uist
dalr	a dale	eg, Coradale (Kari's dale), South Uist
vatn	water	eg, Loch Caravat (Kari's water), North Uist
setr	house/ dwelling	eg, Loch Eashadar (deserted dwelling), North Uist

Some place-names contain personal elements, among which are Balranald and Balmartin, derived from Gaelic 'baile' a township, thus Balranald is Ranald's town. Other names reflect past history such as Balivanich, the town of the monks (Baile a' Mhanaich). Nunton, in Benbecula, echoes the time when a nunnery existed there in medieval times. Kilpheder, South Uist, is the Church of St Peter. Bornish, also in South Uist (Gaelic: Bornais), is the headland of the fort.

As will be appreciated, the study of place-names is fraught with problems, not the least of which is the required intimate knowledge of a particular area, particularly the topography. In addition, a familiarity with Gaelic provides not a few clues to the meaning of a place-name. Some Gaelic words which appear on signposts and maps include:

PLACE-NAME	MEANING	
Aird	height, headland	eg, Aird (height), Benbecula
Baile	township	eg, Baile (town), Eriskay
Beag	small	eg, Keallasay Beg, North Uist
Mor	big	eg, Oitir Mhor (big bank), Barra
Tuath	north	eg, Bagh a Tuath (Northbay), Barra
Alt	stream	eg, Loch Altabrug (stream of the fort), South Uist
Gleann	glen, narrow valley	eg, Ghlinn Dail (Glendale), South Uist

One last name which might excite some interest is that of the mountain on the east side of South Uist, Hecla (1,990ft/606m). There is a conspicuous peak in Iceland bearing the same name, derived from the Norse 'hekla' meaning a cowled garment. One can imagine some Viking sailing down the eastern seaward side of South Uist, marking off the landmarks on a sheet of thinly scraped leather and coming up with an imaginative name for the mountain which reminded him of a cowled monk which he might have seen on one of his raids in the island of Iona. Pure speculation, of course, but one can never quite know with place-name derivations and origins.

FURTHER READING

Angus, S. *The Outer Hebrides: The Shaping Of Islands* (White Horse Press, 1997)

Armit, I. *The Archaeology Of Skye And The Western Isles* (Edinburgh University Press, 1996)

Branigan, K. *Castlebay To Caolis* (Sheffield Academic Press, 1997)

Branigan, K. and Foster, P. *Barra – Archaeological Research On Ben Tangavel* (Sheffield Academic Press, 1995)

Burnett, R. *Benbecula*; (Mingulay Press, Benbecula, 1986)

Charnley, B. *Shipwrecked On Vatersay* (MacLean Press, 1992)

Comunn Eachdraidh Bharraidh *Mingulay – An Island Guide* (Commun Eachraidh Bharraidh, 1994)

Cunningham, P. *Birds Of The Outer Hebrides* (Acair, 1990)

Hunter, J. *The Making Of The Crofting Community* (John Donald, 1976)

MacGregor, M. *Between Two Worlds: Lochmaddy* (Taigh Chearsabhagh, 1996)

MacLeod, F. *The Chapels In The Western Isles* (Acair, 1997)

MacQuarrie, A. *Cille Bharra* (Grant Books, 1989)

Parker, J. *Walks In The Western Isles* (H.M.S.O., 1996)

Thompson, F. *The Uists and Barra* (David & Charles, 1974)

Thompson, F. *Crofting Years* (Luath Press, 1997)

INDEX

Page numbers in *italic* indicate illustrations

Farewell to Barra